Self-Efficacy in Action

Self-Efficacy in Action

Tales from the Classroom for Teaching, Learning, and Professional Development

Edited by Freddie A. Bowles and Cathy J. Pearman

ROWMAN & LITTLEFIELD
Lanham • Boulder • New York • London

Published by Rowman & Littlefield
A wholly owned subsidiary of The Rowman & Littlefield Publishing Group, Inc.
4501 Forbes Boulevard, Suite 200, Lanham, Maryland 20706
www.rowman.com

Unit A, Whitacre Mews, 26-34 Stannary Street, London SE11 4AB

British Library Cataloguing in Publication Information Available

Library of Congress Cataloging-in-Publication Data

Names: Bowles, Freddie A., 1952- editor. | Pearman, Cathy J., editor.
Title: Self-efficacy in action : tales from the classroom for teaching, learning, and professional
  development / edited by Freddie A. Bowles and Cathy J. Pearman.
Description: Lanham, Maryland : Rowman & Littlefield Education, 2017. | Includes bibliographical
  references.
Identifiers: LCCN 2016047568| ISBN 9781475825190 (cloth : alk. paper) | ISBN 9781475825206
  (pbk. : alk. paper)
Subjects: LCSH: Educational psychology. | Teachers--Psychology. | Teachers--In-service training. |
  Teaching--Psychological aspects. | Self-efficacy.
Classification: LCC LB1062.6 .S43 2017 | DDC 370.15--dc23 LC record available at https://
  lccn.loc.gov/2016047568

Printed in the United States of America

This book is dedicated to the amazing teachers and teacher educators whose passion and commitment to making a difference in the lives of children and youth is the very definition of self-efficacy.

Contents

Foreword

I had the privilege of serving as president of the Association of Teacher Educators (ATE) in 2010–2011. By that time, the "Educational Reform" movement was in high gear. Centered around federal legislation such as "No Child Left Behind" and "Race to the Top," there continued to be intense focus on standardized testing accompanied by intense scrutiny of public schools and public school teachers, whose performance evaluations were becoming more and more tied to those standardized test scores. Although less publicized, but no less serious, changes were becoming more and more evident to careful observers:

- more time spent on testing and preparation for testing; less time available for teaching
- almost exclusive focus on the heavily tested content areas of language arts and math
- little time spent on social studies and science; virtual exclusion of art, foreign language, music, and PE
- significant reduction in lunch and recess or activity time for elementary school children, and
- emergence of more scripted or, at least, more standardized curriculum planning.

Along with the many visible results of the "reform" agenda, I began to sense changes in the faces and voices of classroom teachers. The constant criticizing and blaming of teachers in the media seemed to be eroding the pride they had in themselves as teachers and their dedication to teaching and learning. The narrowed curriculum and the loss of autonomy for planning and scheduling in their own classrooms seemed to be eroding their passion and creativity. The cumulative effect of years of this hyper-scrutiny also seemed to be having another devastating effect—the loss of teacher self-efficacy, that is, teachers' beliefs in their own competence in teaching and in making a difference in the lives of children and young people.

The link between the individual teacher's self-efficacy and teaching effectiveness has been well documented. You will see much of that research in this volume, but much of the prior research had been conducted in "quieter" times. With that in mind, as the president of ATE, I appointed the Commission on Teacher Self-Efficacy in 2010 to take a comprehensive look at the broader issue of teacher self-efficacy in the context of the more turbulent era of "Educational Reform."

After five years of comprehensive research and discussion, dozens of conference presentations, and countless hours of writing and editing, the commission offers this volume with the hope of contributing to this most important field of study. I am proud to be associated with the friends and colleagues who have worked so diligently to assemble this volume for the benefit of the greatest profession in the world.

Dr. Terrell M. Peace
Director of Graduate and Undergraduate Teacher Education
Huntington University
President, Association of Teacher Educators, 2010–2011

Preface

In 2010, the president of the Association of Teacher Educators, Terrell M. Peace, formed a commission to investigate and conduct research related to self-efficacy in teaching, learning, and schooling. A natural outgrowth of reflections of this research evolved into a series of in-depth discussions and conference presentations conducted by commission members on how self-efficacy is manifested in teachers and how it is enacted in everyday teaching situations.

As an organization of teacher educators and classroom teachers, we have a special and devoted concern for the development of self-efficacy in educators across all teaching and learning experiences. Consequently, the members of this commission authored this text to share with you the commission's vision of what we wish for all teachers, and their students, everywhere. This vision encapsulates classrooms where teachers are confident decision makers, risk takers, and change agents for the benefit of their students' learning.

This text is organized into ten chapters aligned with standards developed by the Interstate Teacher Assessment and Support Consortium (InTASC) and published by the Council of Chief State School Officers (CCSSO). Each chapter is designed to promote critical thought and drive discussion of what it means to have self-efficacy and what self-efficacy looks like in implementation.

Chapters share the behaviors, thoughts, and processes self-efficacious teachers employ in teaching and learning scenarios. With a common format across chapters that includes an opening vignette illustrating situations that arise in the lives of educators, each chapter concept is then explained along with its application to the vignette. Through discussion, the self-efficacy concept is broadened to help you, the reader, establish the importance and generalizability of the concept. Each chapter concludes with guiding questions, additional resources, and a list of references to facilitate reflection.

As you read this book, we hope you are able to see yourself in the vignettes and use the chapters to reflect on your own self-efficacy. If you are a teacher educator, a classroom teacher, or a teacher candidate, we encourage you to share this information in your classrooms, as professional development, or as models for your future classrooms. Self-efficacious teachers drive changes necessary for the improvement of our education system which, in turn, improves the lives of our children, society, and future.

Thank you for reading and sharing this publication. We wish each of you the best on your journey to becoming a self-efficacious educator.

Freddie A. Bowles, PhD and Cathy J. Pearman, PhD
Co-Editors

Introduction

Nancy P. Gallavan

How can I organize my classroom so every student is excited to attend class, feels welcome, is ready to engage in the learning, and wants to achieve? What can I do to make sure that expectations are clear and feasible for every student? How do I adjust the teaching and learning so every student attains a sense of success and reward? How do I motivate participation, challenge the status quo, enrich critical thinking, and promote individual expression and creativity? What can I do to ensure effective communication with parents to gain their understanding and support?

These probing questions exemplify some of the concerns that many teacher candidates and classroom teachers ask themselves as they begin teaching and continue to grow throughout their professional careers. Focusing their attention on classroom complexities, teachers benefit greatly by expanding their conceptual thinking and developing pedagogical strategies to better meet the needs and interests of each learner.

By increasing awareness and critical consciousness, teachers enhance their self-efficacy. They strengthen their application of the techniques learned through their teacher-education programs and intensify their advocacy for authentic teaching, learning, and schooling through mindful reflecting on their practices.

THE MIEN OF SELF-EFFICACY

Self-efficacy encompasses an individual's beliefs in her or his abilities to achieve a goal (Bandura, 1977; 1997) through multiple dimensions (Skaalvik and Skaalvik, 2007) generating control of four essential areas of being, par-

Skaalvik ; Skaalvik, 2007

ticularly as an educator: motivation, implementation, environment, and negotiations—the MIEN of self-efficacy.

Motivation addresses the question of *why*, offering rationalization and
justifications for our thoughts, beliefs, values, and assumptions based on both
external and internal stimuli. Implementation speaks to the question of *how*,
providing the explanation and clarification for the ways we conduct ourselves when among other people and on our own as well as the ways we treat
ourselves. Environment answers the questions of *who*, *where*, and *when*,
providing the establishment and contextualization of our existence and sense
of place. Negotiations respond to the questions of *what* and *what else*, with
descriptions and explorations delving into the possibilities for mediation,
reconciliation, and balance.

A teacher's sense of motivation, implementation, environment, and negotiations influences the selection of purpose, communications, and setting
associated with pursuing particular outcomes. For example, teachers and
learners benefit when everyone is excited about the upcoming learning experience, engaged in the activities, equipped to access resources and express
outcomes, and empowered to make individual decisions.

These four words—motivation, implementation, environment, and negotiations—start with letters that spell the word *mien*, meaning character and
disposition. Educator preparation programs and standards emphasize the
understanding and demonstration of appropriate professional knowledge,
skills, and dispositions.

While teachers' knowledge and skills are well defined and clearly stipu-
lated in most educator-preparation programs, teachers' dispositions remain
more elusive and undetermined. This text offers a framework for enhancing
teacher self-efficacy centered on one's mien or dispositions associated with
motivation, implementation, environment, and negotiations.

Four Sources of Teacher Self-Efficacy

While teacher educators strive to enhance self-efficacy in teacher candidates
and classroom teachers, the overarching mission of the education enterprise
is for teachers to instill a sense of self-efficacy in their young learners for
lifelong learning in preparation for college, career, community, and civic life.
Each of the four sources of self-efficacy (Bandura, 1997) equips candidates
to recognize the presence and power of self-efficacy in themselves and their
own learners. The four sources of self-efficacy include:

- Mastery Experiences—Experiences where the learner achieves success
  accompanied by satisfaction; this source of self-efficacy is the most robust. Motivation plays an extremely important role in mastery experi-

ences. Learners must be encouraged and engaged honestly with activities connected to them personally.

- Vicarious Experiences—Experiences where the learner observes success in an equally comparable peer; this source of self-efficacy is highly influential. Interactions between and among peers that are natural promote learners' beliefs supporting achievement and implementation.
- Verbal Persuasion—Experiences where the learner hears about success from a credible source coupled with persuasive and productive feedback. Environments with teachers, coaches, mentors, and so on, who guide learners through tasks with authentic cognitive, affective, physical, and social support help advance self-efficacy.
- Emotional State—Experiences where the learner maintains a successful outlook or attitude that energizes the individual and increases one's beliefs. Negotiations that capitalize upon one's strengths further increase one's strengths, especially when teachers work holistically to maximize productivity and minimize pressure.

Multidisciplinary Model of Teacher Efficacy

Tschannen-Moran, Woolfolk Hoy, and Hoy (1998) developed a multidisciplinary model of teacher efficacy. The four sources of efficacy lead to cognitive processing (thoughts, beliefs, values, and assumptions). Then a teacher can both analyze the effectiveness of the teaching and learning via student achievement and assess the effectiveness of the teaching via teacher competence.

The resulting data reveal the teacher's self-efficacy. Essential to this process is the consequence of this revelation; now is the moment for the teacher to make changes to increase learning and achievement, enhance teaching and self-efficacy, and improve the schooling and curricular advancement (Figure I.1).

TRANSFORMATIVE LEARNING THEORY

The process of enhancing teacher self-efficacy in adults parallels Mezirow's Transformative Learning Theory (TLT): "Learning is understood as the process of using *a prior* interpretation to construe a new or revised interpretation of the meaning of one's experience in order to guide future action" (Mezirow, 1996, p. 162) resulting in a "dramatic fundamental change in the way we see ourselves and the world in which we live" (p. 318). TLT consists of a "constructivist, an orientation which holds that the way learners interpret and reinterpret their sense experience, is central to making meaning and hence learning" (Mezirow, 1994, p. 222).

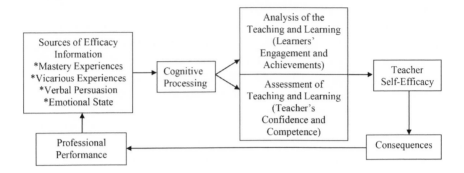

Figure I.1

Mezirow posits that an individual's worldview learning comprises two structures: meaning schemas and meaning perspectives (1991; 2000). Meaning schemas include the many new concepts, vocabulary, principles, and practices that each of us learns through both formal and informal learning experiences. Understanding evolves and expands in new worldviews, but changes in meaning schemas do not prompt transformation.

Once the new worldview is adapted into an individual's life, transformation occurs via meaning perspectives. Meaning perspectives affect all facets of our holistic being incorporating our psychomotor (sensations and perceptions—the individual physical self), psychological (thoughts and feelings—the personal private self), epistemological (knowledge and skills—the responsible capable self), and sociolinguistic (society and language—the social public self) components of our character.

Changes in meaning perspectives prompt transformation in the beliefs we maintain about other people and ourselves. For example, as a person learns the approaches for maintaining a budget that balances income and expenses, most likely that person's meaning schema evolves and expands. However, when a person internalizes the realities associated with balancing budgets contextualized for specific populations such as the working poor, that person experiences transformation in meaning perspectives.

TLT continues by identifying two types of learning that apply to both meaning schemas and meaning perspectives: instrumental and communicative learning. Instrumental learning focuses on gaining technical knowledge by conducting tasks involving inquiry and discovery leading to problem solving. Communicative learning concentrates on adding practical knowledge based on the influences of other people's ideas and experiences. However, only when instrumental learning and communicative learning prompt reflection and action resulting in transformation does the learning apply to meaning perspectives.

Transformation involves three themes: centrality of experience, critical reflection, and rational discourse. In his first theme, Mezirow refers to centrality of experience as a "disorienting dilemma" because the experience does not fit into or match with an individual's prior knowledge or anticipated perception. This type of experience may be epochal, occurring all at once, or it may be incremental, occurring as installments over time. The essential element of the disorienting dilemma is the individual's increased awareness and immediate actions.

Mezirow's second theme of transformation encompasses critical reflection as self-assessment that discloses one's thoughts, beliefs, values, and assumptions related to three areas: critical reflection—describing the current content available about a topic or issue and the ways the content is used; process reflection—deciding the sufficient amount of current content and the methods for obtaining it; and premise reflection—determining the criteria and the reasons for drawing conclusions. Premise reflection is the most important area of self-assessment revealing one's natural inner core, holistic objectivity, honest perseverance, and authentic reflectivity.

The third theme of transformation delves into rational discourse that ideally draws upon complete and accurate information, fair and truthful conversations, genuine and creative openness, and caring and compassionate empathy. Rational discourse empowers an individual to examine events objectively while exchanging similar observations and experiences with others. Reassurance reflected by others strengthens an individual's mien: motivation to explore viable options, interactions to formulate a constructive plan, environment to establish a supportive setting, and negotiations to foster valuable transformation.

ENHANCING SELF-EFFICACY IN LEARNERS

Based on the research of Margolis and McCabe (2006), we offer twelve tips for enhancing self-efficacy in learners (of all ages and at all stages):

1. Organize the learning experience so the expectations, procedures, and assessments are meaningful, relevant, and developmentally appropriate.
2. Invite learners into the learning process by asking intriguing questions, showing captivating photographs, or sharing mysterious artifacts, and so on, so the motivation offers challenge, reward, and personal connection.
3. Facilitate interactions among learners as they share their explorations with one another, watch other learners present their findings, and see

diverse members of their classes and the country's population fulfill various roles and responsibilities.

4. Establish a contemporary and dynamic sense of place in the learning environment (i.e., classroom, lab, gym, etc.) that is comfortable physically, mentally, emotionally, and socially and reflects the learners' contemporary interests.

5. Guide learners with a variety of engaging learning strategies framed by specific parameters yet encouraging expressive creativity; allow learners opportunities for negotiation within a collaboratively generated range of options and outcomes.

6. Get to know each learner so you can build upon each learner's inner strength(s), community connections, and cultural characteristics.

7. Model the power and processes of maintaining an open mind by thinking aloud during problem solving and decision making.

8. Provide individual, specific, and developmentally appropriate feedback equitable for all students (specifically in terms of gender, race, ethnicity, nationality, language, ability, religion, etc.) that is both spoken in class and written on papers, presentations, and projects.

9. Demonstrate the benefits of learning from isolated failures by reviewing and revising a particular part of the process or piece of the product rather than associating failure as a personal trait.

10. Give praise for the effort of working hard and believing in oneself to both individual learners and to groups of learners.

11. Help learners to set their own goals and to monitor and measure their progress toward achievement of the goals.

12. Feature opportunities for learners to reflect upon their progress, to write about their successes, to share their challenges and rewards, and to enjoy the satisfaction of learning.

ORGANIZATION OF THIS TEXT

This text has been organized into ten chapters. Each of the chapters examines a different aspect of teacher self-efficacy aligned with the Interstate Teacher Assessment and Support Consortium (InTASC) standards published by the Council of Chief State School Officers (CCSSO, 2011) (see the appendix). Each aspect of teacher self-efficacy starts with the letter "C" including confidence, care, community, content, creativity, challenge, curriculum, control, collaboration, and collegiality. These ten aspects were selected for their unique roles and important contributions to teacher education.

- Chapter 1 reveals the *Confidence* in twenty-two teacher candidates in a six-week practicum, based on their reviews of lesson plans and summative reflections.
- Chapter 2 uses the characteristics of *Commitment*, Attention, Reflection, and Empathy (CARE) to illustrate how Noddings's research on caring supports self-efficacy studies.
- Chapter 3 discusses the self-efficacy concept of *Community* by contrasting two classroom scenarios through the construct of a Collective Classroom Efficacy model.
- Chapter 4 delves into the impact of self-efficacy on the teaching of *Content*. This chapter expands the discussion across academic, pedagogical, assessment, and learner content.
- Chapter 5 takes the reader into a classroom where one teacher's innovation and *Creativity* resulted in tremendous growth in student achievement.
- Chapter 6 demonstrates how developing one's self-efficacy is dependent upon one's ability to interact with and overcome *Challenge*.
- Chapter 7 reminds us that *Curriculum* is a driving force in our classrooms and is best enacted by teachers with high degrees of self-efficacy. This chapter points out the need for high-quality teachers and effective instructional models.
- Chapter 8 discusses *Control*, especially the concept of locus of control and the effects an increasingly narrowing curriculum have on the self-efficacy of classroom teachers.
- Chapter 9 portrays how one university system's *Collaboration* partnership with neighboring schools impacted teacher practices and efficacy in meeting the needs of students.
- Chapter 10 outlines the struggle, and importance, of maintaining *Collegiality* in the face of increased demands for student achievement and teacher effectiveness.

Each chapter begins with a classroom vignette that introduces one of the "C" aspects followed by a description of the aspect telling what it is, an explanation of the aspect detailing how it applies, a justification of the aspect rationalizing why it is important, and an extrapolation of the aspect broadening the conversation. Each chapter is designed as an inclusive unit with a list of discussion questions, resources, and references so that readers may utilize the individual chapters as needed. The book closes with final thoughts from the editors.

ATE COMMISSION ON TEACHER SELF-EFFICACY

This text is authored by the members of the Association of Teacher Educators (ATE) Commission on Teacher Self-Efficacy and their co-authors. Appointed by ATE president Terrell M. Peace in 2010, active members of the commission and their respected institutions include:

Jennifer G. Beasley; University of Arkansas
Glenda L. Black; Nipissing University, Ontario, Canada
Freddie A. Bowles; University of Arkansas
Molly Funk; Core School Solutions, LLC
Nancy P. Gallavan; University of Central Arkansas
Elizabeth Johnson; Eastern Michigan University
Shirley Lefever-Davis; Wichita State University
Jane Manner; Eastern Carolina University
Terrell Peace; Huntington University
Cathy J. Pearman; Missouri State University
Walt Polka; Niagara University
Bianca Prather-Jones; Northern Kentucky University
LeAnn Putney; University of Nevada, Las Vegas
V. Carole Smith; Arkansas Tech University
Kathy Walsh; Eastern Michigan University
Elizabeth K. Ward; Texas Wesleyan University
Angela Webster-Smith; University of Central Arkansas
Steven K. Wojcikiewicz; Oregon State University
William Young; Oglala Lakota College

APPRECIATION

As members of the ATE Commission on Teacher Self-Efficacy, we appreciate the wealth of opportunities afforded us to read, research, talk, present, and write about teacher self-efficacy to enhance our own self-efficacy as teacher educators and to contribute to the practices advocated and the resources available in teacher education. As teacher candidates and classroom teachers, you are encouraged to immerse yourself into this text to enhance your self-efficacy and the efficacy of your young learners.

REFERENCES

Bandura, A. (1977). Self-efficacy: Toward a unifying theory of behavioral change. *Psychological Review, 84*, 191–215.
Bandura, A. (1997). *Self-efficacy: The exercise of control*. New York: Freeman.
Margolis, H., & McCabe, P. (2006). Improving self-efficacy and motivation: What to do, what to say. *Intervention in School and Clinic, 41*(4), 218–27.

Mezirow, J. (1991). *Transformative Dimensions of Adult Learning.* San Francisco, CA: Jossey-Bass.

Mezirow, J. (1994). Understanding transformation theory. *Adult Education Quarterly, 44*(4), 222–32.

Mezirow, J. (1996). Contemporary paradigms of learning. *Adult Education Quarterly, 46*(3), 158–73.

Mezirow, J. (2000). *Learning as Transformation: Critical Perspectives on a Theory in Progress.* San Francisco, CA: Jossey-Bass.

Skaalvik, E. M., & Skaalvik, S. (2007). Dimensions of teacher self-efficacy and relations with strain factors, perceived collective teacher efficacy, and teacher burnout. *Journal of Educational Psychology, 99*, 611–25.

Tschannen-Moran, M., & Woolfolk Hoy, A. (2001). Teacher efficacy: Capturing an elusive construct. *Teaching and Teacher Education, 17*, 783–805.

Chapter One

I Was Successful!

Developing Teacher Candidates' Confidence and Self-Efficacy through Reflection and Supervising-Teacher Support

Glenda L. Black

In my last week of placement in my grade 10 History class, there is a lesson that I will carry with me forever, as it was exactly what I hope to accomplish in many more lessons throughout my teaching career. I planned a coopera-tive learning activity of a Paris Peace Conference simulation for groups of five. I planned out the learning goals and roles for the simulation (for assess-ment the students create their own Treaty, which we would compare to the real Treaty of Versailles for consolidation).

I was nervous the students would not do the research and be unprepared for the simulation. On the day of the simulation, the students came prepared and excited. During the simulation, they were engaged, and the critical thinking that occurred during their mock conferences was incredible.

They were well-organized and stayed in their roles the entire class! They were respectful of each other. They knew my rules and expectations when it came to group work, and this showed as they all stayed on task and were all contributing to their groups. I set high expectations for the students and they exceeded them!

When I suggested to my supervising teacher what I wanted to do, she said that I was taking a risk, but believed I was capable of the challenge. I taught to many intelligences and the activity was fun. This should be what teaching is like as much as possible.

This lesson made me feel competent and confident as a teacher and taught me that in my future classroom, I will place emphasis on cooperation,

1

collaboration, interactive activities, engaged learners, and critical thinking. Many students said, "That was fun," or "I enjoyed that," showing me that school can be fun for the students and me! (Casey, teacher candidate, 2013)

Casey described a situation where she felt confident as a teacher. Teachers' confidence and competence is integral to improving students' academic performance (Bangs and Frost, 2012; OECD, 2011). Self-efficacy gives teachers the confidence to effectively develop curriculum and respond to the social and emotional well-being of their students (Bandura 2007; Hoy and Spero, 2005).

Educator-preparation programs, which are the foundation to the development of teachers entering the classroom, have the potential to enhance teacher candidates' self-efficacy and confidence. The present study offers insights into teacher candidates' development toward confidence and provides recommendations for educator-preparation programs regarding how confidence can be fostered and enhanced in teacher candidates. Before a detailed description of the results is discussed, an overview of the theoretical framework and the methodology for the research is presented.

THEORETICAL FRAMEWORK

Teacher Self-Efficacy

Teacher self-efficacy is defined as a teacher's confidence in his or her ability to affect and promote student learning (Bandura, 2007; Dembo & Gibson, 1985; Hoy, 2000). Similarly, researchers (Tschannen-Moran & Woolfolk Hoy, 2001) claim that self-efficacy gives teachers the confidence to inspire their students to achieve their potential and increase their own teaching aspirations. High levels of self-efficacy positively correlate with student achievement (Ashton & Webb, 1986; Leithwood, 2006; Moore & Esselman, 1992; Gibson & Dembo, 1984).

The impact of teacher confidence on student achievement can be explained "as an expression of confidence that one's actions may lead to success and mastery over one-self and have a positive influence on others" (Bordelon et al., 2012, p. 15). Hoy (2000) suggests teacher candidates' development of a lasting sense of efficacy has implications for the future students of the teacher candidates who become early-career teachers. If teacher candidates feel confident to solve problems, they are more motivated to persist in the future (Yost, 2006).

Concerns-Based Model

Fuller's (1969) concerns-based model of teacher development is best described as "perhaps the most classic of stage theories in that it was meant to be relatively invariant, sequential and hierarchical" (Richardson and Placier, 2001, p. 910). In her investigation of beginning teachers she posited a "three phase developmental conceptualization of teachers' concerns" (Fuller, 1969, p. 221). The three stages advanced from (1) pre-teaching—no-concern to (2) early teaching—concerns with self to (3) late teaching—concerns with pupils (Fuller, 1969). By the mid-1970s Fuller and Brown (1975) revised the developmental stages as progressing from (1) concerns about self to (2) concerns about tasks or situations to (3) concerns about impact on students.

Conway and Clark (2003) extended the concerns-based model by proposing that teacher candidates progressed on an outward journey following the three stages of development (Fuller & Brown, 1975) and on an inward journey of self-development. The inward journey focuses the teacher candidates' attention on their "self-as-teacher," as related to their hopes and fears (Conway & Clark, 2003, p. 470). Insight into one's self is achieved through reflection.

Reflective Practice

Support for reflective practice is clearly evidenced in the literature (Larivee, 2008; Smith, 2011). Reflecting on practice is a strategy for self-evaluation and making judgments on knowledge and capacity. According to Boyd and Fales (1983), "reflective learning is the process of internally examining and exploring an issue of concern, triggered by an experience, which creates and clarifies meaning in terms of self, and which results in a changed conceptual perspective" (p. 100).

Depending on their development as a teacher, candidates' concerns are related to self, tasks or situations, or impact on students (Fuller & Brown, 1975; Putney & Broughton, 2010) activated during their mastery experience (teaching practicum). Bandura (1986) supported self-reflection as it positively contributes to altering a person's thinking and actions. Fundamental to the concept of self-efficacy is the ability to self-reflect, evaluate the situation, and develop a plan for action using one's skills and knowledge (Bandura, 1989).

METHOD

The study followed a qualitative research design to provide rich description and in-depth insight into the factors that influence teacher candidates' development toward self-efficacy and confidence.

The participants in the study were twenty-two teacher candidates (sixteen female and six male) from the same teacher-preparation program, in their final semester. All the teacher candidates were pursuing qualifications in the intermediate-senior divisions (grades seven through twelve). The sample represents a range of teaching experiences: rural, urban, public, Catholic, First Nations, elementary, and secondary schools.

Data were collected over a three-month period and included the participants' lesson plans with recorded reflections from their six weeks of practicum followed by four weeks of instruction on campus. The data included the teacher candidates' open-ended impressions and feelings around their practical experiences and their perceptions of confidence in their teaching practice.

During the six-week practicum, the teacher candidates recorded their reflections directly on their lesson plans by reflecting on what went well, what they were able to achieve, and how their learning would influence future situations.

Following the practicum, the teacher candidates created a summative reflection by reviewing their lesson plan reflections and noting changes in themselves. They also described when or if they felt confident as a classroom teacher.

Methods of data analysis (i.e., lesson plan reflections and summative reflections) included the three streams of activity identified by Miles and Huberman (1994) including (a) data reduction (reviewed the data, developed and coded data to summarize, sort, and organize); (b) data display (organized and compressed data into a matrix); and (c) conclusion drawing/verification (made meaning of the data by noting patterns, interpretations, and triangulating sources).

RESULTS

Twenty of the twenty-two candidates stated that by the end of the last practicum for the program, they felt confident as a teacher. The two candidates who did not perceive themselves as confident believed more experience was necessary.

Parker, one of the two candidates, explained, *"Examining my reflections you can see some changes over time. In many areas I have achieved a great deal of success, but there are a great deal of areas that still require significant improvement."* He continued by explaining, *"I would liken this to musical achievement in many respects. Although through practicing and performing, you can notice notable and quantifiable improvement, you are never fully satisfied, and grow pickier with your abilities as you improve."*

The remaining twenty candidates felt confident as a teacher at some point during their practicum. Based on their lesson plans and summative reflections, four themes emerged as the situation or condition where the teacher candidates identified themselves as confident: (1) effective classroom management, (2) successful curriculum planning and implementation, (3) rapport development with students, and/or (4) supervising-teacher approval.

The candidates' cognitive development improved, as evidenced in their use of reflection to put theory into practice; affective changes were dependent on the situation: candidates' comfort with content, planning, students, or classroom management. Pseudonyms were used in place of the teacher candidates' names.

Classroom Management

All teacher candidates reflected on classroom management. The differences included the type of management issues, student involvement as whole class or individual, and how the candidates approached the challenge.

For example, early in her placement, Ariel believed she needed to be a friend to her high school students, especially disruptive students. She explained, "*I used to be a pushover for the sake of being liked by my students. I learned that intervention strategies that are firm, yet fair for classroom management, are absolutely necessary to counteract the actions of disruptive students.*"

The teacher candidates progressed in their teacher development to recognize the connection between classroom management and curriculum planning and implementation, "*I have learned that the more engaged the students are in the lesson, the less likely they will misbehave*" (Adrien). Similarly, Casey simultaneously planned engaging lessons and behavior expectations, as the students "*knew her [my] rules and expectations when it came to group work.*"

Curriculum Planning and Implementation

Casey's history lesson clearly reflected her emphasis on curriculum planning and implementation, "*This lesson made me feel competent and confident as a teacher and taught me that in my future classroom I will place emphasis on cooperation, collaboration, interactive activities, engaged learners, and critical thinking.*"

Similarly, all the teacher candidates' lesson plans showed they were differentiating their instruction (i.e., inquiry method, cooperative learning, various groupings, and multiple intelligences for planning instruction and assessment, and so on) to meet the learning needs of their students.

The level of concern about their planning and instruction was dependent on the teacher candidates' expertise in the content area. For example, "*At first my main focus was the content I was teaching. I concentrated so hard on making good lessons, but I found it hard to be creative in the math classroom as well as learn the content.*"

Chris continued to explain, "*I was learning and teaching the content, filling in the lesson plans, and managing classroom behavior. I was strug-*

gling to get through." Cam, with a music license, said honestly, "*I was completely out of my element teaching Geography, Math, and a little bit of Art.*"

The teacher candidates' confidence and self-efficacy were linked to the students' learning, engagement, and assessment. For example, "*I enjoyed interacting with the students and keeping them engaged in the content.*"

Kim continued by explaining, "*When it came to marking their tests, I had a lot of pride when I discovered the whole class got over 80% on the osmosis section of the quiz.*" Kelly experienced confidence in her teaching through her students' success after she administered an assessment her supervising teacher thought was too hard, "*I did give that test to the grade nine science class and they had an average of 88%. I had taught the material effectively, students had a solid understanding of the concepts, and I was successful in engaging them.*"

Rapport with Students

All the teacher candidates' lesson plan reflections indicated a concern about persevering with individual students with academic or behavioral issues. For some of the candidates, the establishment of rapport or making connections with students at risk was their indicator of teaching confidence.

Reese, whose supervising teacher was a guidance counselor, described her "*unbelievable experience*" when a student at risk requested to speak specifically to her. "*He took the advice and the encouragement I said to him to heart and I could tell he truly looked up to me as a role model.*"

Robin described a number of "*moments*" with students. A situation with her grade nine science class with an at-risk student who was "*frequently off task and would complete few assignments*" struck her as significant when the student directed other students to "*be quiet, I'm listening to Ms. Riley.*"

In their summative reflections, the teacher candidates reflected on how their teacher development progressed from a focus on their teaching to their impact on students. For example Rene stated, "*After reviewing my reflections from my six-week placement, over time . . . I focused a lot in my reflections on how I interacted with students, and less about my teaching methods.*"

Supervising Teacher

None of the teacher candidates' lesson plan reflections recorded concerns about their supervising teacher, which is not surprising because the supervising teachers reviewed their lesson plans. Additionally, supervising teachers were required to evaluate the teacher candidate's performance, and the candidates did not want to influence their evaluation by commenting on their supervising teacher.

Nevertheless, the candidates' summative reflections, which were not reviewed by the supervising teacher, revealed that the supervising teacher's approval directly influenced their confidence as a teacher. For example, Mitch stated, "*My second placement went waaaay better! I was comfortable with my supervising teacher; she was a hard worker but also very realistic so I wasn't as intimidated.*"

Casey described support from her supervising teacher as believing "*I was capable of the challenge.*" Mel, another candidate stated, "*My supervising teacher was very honest about my strengths and weaknesses, and gave me ample feedback on a daily basis. This constant dialogue really helped boost my confidence levels and helped me to excel as a teacher.*"

DISCUSSION AND CONCLUSION

The results from this study further corroborate the literature on teacher self-efficacy, so much that teacher candidates who perceived themselves as confident created engaging learning environments for their students (Bordelon et al., 2012; Tschannen-Moran & Woolfolk Hoy, 2001; Yost, 2006).

The teacher candidates described in detail the teaching and learning they developed and implemented, which was creative and innovative and met the needs of their learners. For example, Casey identified her history lesson as the first moment she felt confident as a teacher. She planned her "instruction that supported[s] every student in meeting rigorous learning goals" (InTASC Standard #7: Planning for Instruction) by preparing her students for the critical-thinking learning opportunity (treaty simulation) (CCSSO, 2011, p. 8).

Although the concerns or challenges of the teacher candidates could be categorized as self, task, and students (Fuller & Brown, 1975), the responses from the teacher candidates go beyond the academic learning of the students. All the teacher candidates referred to students at risk and problem solved how to reach these students beyond their academic needs to meeting their learners' social and emotional needs.

Using the concerns-based model of teachers' development (Fuller and Brown, 1975), Casey progressed to the highest stage, as she was concerned about her impact on students. By "designing[s] and implementing[s] developmentally appropriate and challenging learning experiences," she met InTASC Standard #1: Learners Development (CCSSO, 2011, p. 9).

A significant factor influencing the teacher candidates' development was the support or lack of support from their supervising teacher. Praise, when appropriate, and detailed descriptive feedback from their supervising teacher strongly influenced the development of self-efficacy and confidence.

To assist teacher candidates in their development toward confidence and teacher self-efficacy, the following recommendations for teacher preparation programs and supervising teachers are based on the results from the current study and literature on teacher self-efficacy and confidence, teacher developmental concerns, and reflection.

Develop Reflection Skills

Teacher-preparation program faculty and supervising teachers are encouraged to provide explicit instruction on reflection skills to heighten candidates' awareness of the complexity of teaching and student learning and behavior (Putney & Broughton, 2010). By developing their reflective skills, teacher candidates are more likely to progress beyond stating past experiences of a journal-style of writing and move toward identifying problems and developing action plans for future lessons, with the goal of increasing confidence in their teaching.

Introducing a reflection framework will assist teacher candidates to self-assess and enhance their understanding of their progression through the levels of reflection, with the goal of empowering the teacher candidates (Nolan & Sim, 2011). An extension to the reflection self-analysis framework is to enhance teacher candidates' understanding that teacher development toward confidence and self-efficacy is a normal process that requires knowledge and practice. Teacher preparation programs need to establish criteria for assessing critical reflection (Larivee, 2008; Smith, 2011).

The intersection of reflection skills and the stages of teacher development could assist teacher candidates in understanding their development toward confidence and self-efficacy. Although some argue that assessing reflection stifles authentic reflective practice (Beveridge, 1997; Sumsion & Fleet, 1996), a measure is still necessary to assist candidates in their self-assessment and provide teacher-preparation-program faculty and teacher supervisors with a developmental scale to provide descriptive feedback for critical reflection.

Understanding Stages of Teacher Development

Assisting teachers-in-training to understand that the process of moving from self to task, to students (Fuller & Brown, 1975), which develops into confidence and self-efficacy, is normal. Teacher candidates using reflection will be able to self-assess their progress toward self-efficacy.

Supervising Teacher and Teacher Candidate Relationship

The relationship between the teacher candidate and supervising teacher and subsequent comments and feedback had a powerful effect on the teacher candidates' confidence and self-efficacy and especially on their affective outcome, a "change in attitude or emotional state" (Nolan & Sim, 2011, p.

124). For all the teacher candidates in this study, feelings of confidence and self-efficacy were dependent on the affirmation or criticism of their supervising teacher.

The teacher candidates frequently questioned their ability to be a teacher or their ability to be a successful teacher. The teacher candidates' reflections showed frustration and doubt with their knowledge and skills. Supervising teachers have the potential to inspire confidence through their support and words of encouragement for motivation and descriptive feedback on how to improve their teaching practice.

Casey was as excited about the history lesson as her students, *"Many students said, 'That was fun,' or 'I enjoyed that,' showing me that school can be fun for the students and me!"* With the support of her supervising teacher, her reflections assisted her in developing an awareness of her confidence as a teacher as she progressed from concerns about herself to concerns about her students.

QUESTIONS TO CONSIDER FOR TEACHER CANDIDATES, SUPERVISING TEACHERS, AND EDUCATION FACULTY

1. What might you see and hear that tells you teacher candidates have reached self-efficacy?
2. What are some of the things you are going to do to enhance teacher-candidate self-efficacy? What challenges do you anticipate?
3. What decisions or adjustments might you make along the way toward developing teacher-candidate self-efficacy?
4. How has this conversation about teacher development, reflection, and self-efficacy supported (or not supported) your thinking?
5. What might you (teacher candidate/supervising teacher/faculty) need to do to be best prepared for developing candidates' concern from self to student?
6. Over what factors might you (teacher candidate/supervising teacher/faculty) have the most control for teacher-candidate self-efficacy? Of the elements you can influence, which might have the greatest effect?
7. What might be the primary value of reflection to teacher candidates' self-efficacy?

REFERENCES

Ashton, P. T., & Webb, R. B. (1986). *Teacher efficacy and student achievement.* New York, NY: Longman.

Bandura, A. (1986). *Social foundations of thought and action: A social cognitive theory.* Englewood Cliffs, NJ: Prentice-Hall.

Bandura, A. (1989). Human agency in social cognitive theory. *American Psychologist, 44*(9), 1175–84.

Bandura, A. (2007). Much ado over a faulty conception for perceived self-efficacy grounded in faulty experimentation. *Journal of Social and Clinical Psychology, 26*(6), 641–58.

Bangs, J., & Frost, D. (2012). Teacher self-efficacy, voice and leadership: Towards a poly framework for education international. Education International Research Institute, University of Cambridge Faculty of Education. Retrieved from http://www.educ.cam.ac.uk/centres/lfl/researchanddevelopment/policy/cambridgeseminars/teacher_self-efficacy_voice_leadership.pdf.

Beveridge, I. (1997). Teaching your students to think reflectively: The case for reflective journals. *Teaching in Higher Education, 2*(1), 33–42.

Bordelon, T. D., Phillips, I., Parkison, P. T., Thomas, J., & Howell, C. (2012). Teacher efficacy: How teachers rate themselves and how students rate their teachers. *Action in Teacher Education, 34*(1), 14–25.

Boyd, E. M., & Fales, A. W. (1983). Reflective learning key to learning from experience. *Journal of Humanistic Psychology, 23*(2), 99–117.

Conway, P. F., & Clark, C. M. (2003). The journey inward and outward: A re-examination of Fuller's concerns-based model of teacher development. *Teaching and Teacher Education, 19*, 465–82.

Council of Chief State School Officers (CCSSO). (2011). *Interstate teacher assessment and support consortium (InTASC) model core teaching standards: A resource for state dialogue.* Washington, DC: CCSSO. Retrieved from http://www.ccsso.org/documents/2011/intasc_model_core_teaching_standards_2011.pdf.

Dembo, M. H., & Gibson, S. (1985). Teachers' sense of efficacy: An important factor in school improvement. *The Elementary School Journal, 86*(2), 173–84.

Fuller, F. F. (1969). Concerns of teachers: A developmental conceptualization. *American Educational Research Journal, 6*(2), 207–26.

Fuller, F. F., & Brown, O. H. (1975). Becoming a teacher. In K. Ryan (Ed.), *Teacher education: 74th yearbook of the National Society of Education* (pp. 25–52). Chicago, IL: University of Chicago Press.

Gibson, M. H., & Dembo, M. (1984). Teacher efficacy: A construct validation. *Journal of Education Psychology, 76*(4), 569–82.

Hoy, A. W. (2000). *Changes in teacher efficacy during the early years of teaching.* Paper presented at the annual meeting of the American Educational Research Association, New Orleans, LA.

Hoy, A. W., & Spero, R. B. (2005). Changes in teacher efficacy during the early years of teaching: A comparison of four measures. *Teaching and Teacher Education, 21*(4), 343–56.

Larivee, B. (2008). Development of a tool to assess teachers' level of reflective practice. *Reflective Practice, 9*(3), 341–60.

Leithwood, K. (2006). *Teacher working conditions that matter: Evidence for change.* Toronto, ON: Elementary Teachers' Federation of Ontario.

Miles, M. B., & Huberman, A. M. (1994). *Qualitative data analysis* (2nd ed.). Thousand Oaks, CA: Sage.

Moore, W. P., & Esselman, M. E. (1992). *Teacher efficacy, empowerment, and focused instructional climate: Does student achievement benefit?* Paper presented at the annual meeting of the American Educational Research Association, San Francisco, CA.

Nolan, A., & Sim, J. (2011). Exploring and evaluating levels of reflection in pre-service early childhood teachers. *Australasian Journal of Early Childhood, 36*(3), 122–30.

Organization for Economic Co-operation and Development (OECD). (2011). *Building a high quality teaching profession—Lessons from around the world. Background report for the international summit on the teaching profession.* Paris, FR: OECD. Retrieved from http://www.oecd.org/fr/edu/scolaire/programmeinternationalpourlesuividesacquisdeselevespisa/buildingahigh-qualityteachingprofessionlessonsfromaroundtheworld.htm.

Putney, L. G., & Broughton, S. (2010). Developing teacher efficacy through reflection: A Vygotskian perspective. *Critical Issues in Teacher Education, XVII*, 4–17

Richardson, V., & Placier, P. (2001). Teacher change. In V. Richardson (Ed.), *Handbook of Research on Teaching* (4th ed.) (pp. 905–47). Washington, DC: American Educational Research Association.

Smith, E. (2011). Teaching critical reflection. *Teaching in Higher Education, 16*(2), 211–23.

Sumsion, J., & Fleet, A. (1996). Reflection: Can we assess it? Should we assess it? *Assessment and Evaluation in Higher Education, 21*(2), 121–30. doi:10.1080/0260293960210202.

Tschannen-Moran, M., & Woolfolk Hoy, A. (2001). Teacher efficacy: Capturing an elusive construct. *Teaching and Teacher Education, 17*(7), 783–805. doi:10.1016/S0742-051X(01)00036-1.

Yost, D. Y. (2006). Reflection and self-efficacy: Enhancing retention of qualified teachers from a teacher education perspective. *Teacher Education Quarterly, 33*(4), 59–76.

Chapter Two

Enhancing Efficacy with the Disposition of Care

Angela Webster-Smith

Although this was her first year of high school, Fay thought this would be much like all of her other years of matriculating at the lowest achieving urban schools in her city. As you might guess, her family lived among others who shared a low socioeconomic status; however, Fay's dreams of a college degree and even a PhD remained alive in her heart.

Her first-grade teacher, Mrs. Mathis, believed in her and encouraged her to pursue education as the cornerstone of her future. Unfortunately, most other teachers along her journey had either not noticed the spark in her eyes that learning elicited or simply refrained from acting on it. Her grades ranged from good to excellent and, aside from talking too much, Fay's conduct was commendable. Nonetheless, when it was time to select her high school curriculum, she selected the vocational track.

Fay was following the advice of her mother who served as the only African American secretary in a large corporation. This was a great achievement for her mother, Dot, so Dot steered her daughter down a similar path. After the first reporting period of Mr. Feldman's economics class, he noticed that Fay was the highest achiever among all six periods of his economics classes. His curiosity compelled him to investigate her academic history with the school counselor. After that, he asked Fay to stay after class, much to her fright as she thought she was in trouble somehow.

Feldman proceeded to tell her that she should be more watchful when completing the math portions of his assignments. Besides that, he said, "You are smart." Fay turned her head slightly not quite knowing how to respond to this revelation. This was the first time anyone had ever told her that she was smart. She would continue to ponder these words in her heart because in her world, obedience and compliance were the qualities that people noticed and complimented, not smarts.

Mr. Feldman also asked why a smart girl like her was not on the college track. Fay expressed that she wanted to go to college, but her parents were clear about not having the funds for college. He rebutted that she should never reduce any dream based on current conditions.

The next time that Mr. Feldman asked to see Fay after class was to announce her new schedule. He had persuaded the school counselor to place Fay on the college track, with the exception of one clerical course per semester. He advised Fay that the college track was where she belonged. After the holiday break, Fay's new schedule commenced. Today, Fay holds a PhD.

Mr. Feldman demonstrated CARE in several ways. In turn, his CARE enhanced his efficacy in serving students who were absent any academic legacy. He showed *commitment* to Fay by noticing her potential and by going beyond the call of duty to investigate her story. He gave Fay the requisite *attention* she needed that included affirming her academic potential and working with other school personnel to navigate her curriculum.

Mr. Feldman *reflected* upon his belief system as it pertained to changing society through education, in general, and Fay's life, in particular. Mr. Feldman also displayed *empathy* for Fay's family, her current situation, as well as her future by constructing a schedule that would better prepare her for college yet honor the values of her family. With Mr. Feldman's CARE, this year would not be the same as usual. To the contrary, Mr. Feldman made Fay feel visible, valued, and validated. More importantly, he changed the trajectory of her life.

The community entrusts its children to the care of educators. Dictionary meanings of care propose a variety of impressions such as *temporary keeping*, *protection*, and *discharge of duty*, (www.dictionary.com). Other descriptions for care include *a watchful oversight*, a *lack of negligence,* and the *reasonable person standard* (www.thefreedictionary.com). A more comprehensive characterization of caring is *a set of relational practices that foster mutual recognition and realization, growth, development, protection, empowerment, human community, culture, and possibility* (Gordon, Benner, & Noddings, 1996).

In essence, parents, guardians, and caregivers send or take their children to school for temporary keeping, under the watchful oversight of educators who will protect their children, discharge their professional duty, refrain from negligence, uphold the standard of a prudent educator, and maintain a positive learning environment.

Bipartisan public officials across the nation agree. According to the Council of Chief State School Officers (CCSSO, 2013), care is a professional disposition that must be consistently demonstrated in the work of educators, especially as it pertains to the learning environment. For instance, CCSSO (2013), by way of its InTASC Standard #3 (learning environments), declares that creating a positive learning environment is a core teaching standard.

The expectation for teachers is to create environments that support active engagement in learning, self-motivation, and positive social interaction. CCSSO (2008), through its educational leadership policy standards (ISLLC), proclaims that educational leaders should likewise promote the success of all students by advocating, nurturing, and sustaining a positive school culture. In order to achieve either of the aforementioned, educators must possess self-efficacy to the degree that it is present in their critical dispositions and attending performance, much like Mr. Feldman, who, through the values of caring, advanced his efficacy by advocating for Fay.

A visit to any paragon classroom or school will verify that care is among the professional dispositions of a great educator. Teaching is more than disseminating information, and the school is more than society's holding place for youth while their parents are at work or at play. While the eventual objective of classrooms and schools is academic achievement, much more is involved in student development.

According to Husu and Tirri (2012), schools cannot afford to maintain a singular focus on the delivery of the academic curriculum. A broader outcome is required. To obtain far-reaching objectives, educators must approach the holistic development of students with *commitment*, they must give students proper *attention*, they must engage students with proactive and responsive *reflection*, and they must express *empathy*. Essentially, educators must CARE.

Our nation's achievement history with minoritized and marginalized students shows that high-needs students, even more than others, require teacher efficacy. Teachers have teaching degrees, a license, and a myriad of professional-development sessions to enhance their teacher efficacy. In spite of this, the fact remains that some students are severely underserved. This chapter proposes that teachers move beyond their traditional methods for increasing self-efficacy by employing the tenets of care, much like Mr. Feldman.

CONCEPTUAL FRAMEWORK

Bandura (1977), the father of the theoretical framework for self-efficacy, asserted that educators must believe that their actions will lead to certain outcomes. This efficacy expectation is the "conviction that one can successfully execute the behavior required to produce the outcome" (Bandura, 1977, p. 193). In essence, educator efficacy is the belief in one's ability to influence the learning and behavior of learners, in the same way Mr. Feldman believed he could make a difference in Fay's life.

blame

Efficacy deteriorates to the degree that educators adopt an external locus of control and attribute student failure to outward factors such as the students' background, culture, parents/guardians/caregivers, socioeconomic status, and zip code. A recent study corroborates that efficacy is borne out in the educator's beliefs, thoughts, feelings, words, actions, habits, and ultimately their character toward students and their students' possibilities (Webster-Smith, 2014). Hence, self-efficacy is important for educators to believe in their capabilities to influence student achievement and student behavior positively; otherwise, they are unlikely to perform with care.

The care theory begins with the construct of connection. Therefore, a substantive connection leads to a caring relation that generates caring encounters (Noddings, 2008). Since education is a constellation of encounters (Noddings, 2002) that promote personal and academic development, care should be a natural part of what educators do.

Noddings (1984) purports that caring is basic in the life of humans and that all people want to be cared for; consequently, care is a fundamental aspect of education. For instance, in order for an educator to enhance his or her efficacy, the educator or the "carer" (i.e., the one caring) must be willing to implement a relational approach to schooling and to students, the "cared for" (i.e., the ones receiving the care) (Noddings, 2002).

Mr. Feldman enhanced his self-efficacy by stretching himself to initiate a conversation about the hopes and dreams of his student. Without initiating that after-class conversation, would Fay have passed his class and even graduated from high school? The answer is a resounding yes! The real question is this: Would he have changed her life forever?

It is important to note that caring for someone is different from caring about someone. Caring about someone could be benign neglect (Noddings, 1984) in that a person can care about the victim of a tragedy, for instance, offer a donation, and then move on with her life. In this sense, caring about someone can be empty, as it does not lead to a caring relation. It has some positives, nonetheless, as it can serve as an impetus for genuine care.

On the other hand, caring for someone is richer in that it includes a relational and empathic understanding between the carer and the cared-for, which results in the carer's energy flowing toward the cared-for in ways that the cared for notices and approves (Hansen, 1998). Caring involves specific acts that are the outpouring of the carer's heart (Noddings, 2002). A critical feature of caring, then, is that the cared-for must recognize that an act of caring has, indeed, occurred. When Fay learned that Mr. Feldman changed her schedule, there was no doubt in her mind that he cared. In effect, he had taken action that no one else had dared to take.

A significant hallmark of a caring relationship is dialogue: the carer listens to the expressed needs of the cared-for (Noddings, 2002). Although educators often extrapolate what they believe are the needs of their students, as much as possible, caring teachers respond to the expressed needs of the students. Mr. Feldman clearly listened to Fay to hear of her unrelenting desire to graduate college. He also listened for the values of her family.

Signposts of care in schools manifest as smiles, sighs of relief, and the energetic pursuit of academic endeavors (Noddings, 2008). Care is also evident in the fireworks of illuminations and enlightenments throughout the school. For instance, caring educators look for the topics and issues that might spark a light in the eyes of their students. Noticing such glimmers gives educators ideas about the passions of their students. The proverbial "twinkle in the eye" just might provide insight into what would engage students enough to pursue higher education for their life's work.

With such pronouncements about care, one can see that such indicators could possibly translate into better attendance, positive school culture, more seemly behavior, and greater student achievement. After all, teacher efficacy is the belief that one is responsible for enough variables to make a positive change on the outcomes of children.

Several researchers studied the construct of care in schools with general student populations (Gholami & Tirri, 2012; Noddings, 2007; Noddings, 1999; Noddings, 1992) as well as with African American children (Knight-Diop, 2010; Shevalier & McKenzie, 2012; Siddle Walker, 1996a), and with Latino children (Antrop-Gonzalez & De Jesus, 2006). The philosophy of care attends to academic, social, and emotional factors—essential components necessary to address the needs of students. The ethic of care in schooling is characterized by institutional structures of care in addition to interpersonal structures of care (Siddle Walker, 1996b). Institutional structures of care are evident in the written ethos of the school as well as in staff expectations, an academically rigorous environment, viable postsecondary preparation and advisement, school-family relationships, and a wide variety of co-curricular opportunities (Knight-Diop, 2010). A good exhibition of the practice of institutional structures is that Mr. Feldman was able to collaborate with the school counselor and other teachers to change Fay's schedule to offer a more academically challenging curriculum and at the same time uphold the school-family relationship.

Interpersonal structures of care attend to the academic, social, and psychological needs of students as depicted in the daily interactions that occur within the school: principal-teacher, teacher-teacher, principal-student, teacher-student, and student-student relationships. Examples of positive interpersonal structures are the relationships between Mr. Feldman and the school counselor and other teachers as well as his blossoming rapport with Fay.

In a similar way, the term *caring teaching* is a conceptual framework commonly used to gain insight into the comprehensive nature of teaching (Gholami & Tirri, 2012). Typically discussed dualistically, the term *caring teaching* embraces the labels of personal care and academic care (Goldstein & Lake, 2000; Isenbarger & Zembylas, 2006; Vogt, 2002). The chief intention of academic care is a focus on intellectual enhancement.

At the heart of personal care is the regard for nurturing the whole child. While the caring teacher has more moral and emotional orientations than technical and methodological, he or she aspires to nurture the whole child, including the child's character and dignity (Gholami and Tirri, 2012). In a caring, learning environment, educators offer fun, fairness, and friendship (ibid.). For the sake of clarity, *caring is not built on an emotion-laden practice characterized by low expectations motivated by taking pity on students' social circumstances* (Anthrop-Gonzalez & De Jesus, 2006, p. 411).

So, how does one know the difference between pity and care? Pity is a function of the emotions, whereas care is a derivative of the heart and administered in the service of the heart. Accordingly, caring teachers practice from a heart of compassion.

Pity meets or pacifies the current need of students but does not take the appropriate action that moves them toward a promising future. Pity does not yield improvement, whereas care refuses to leave students in a less powerful position than they were found in. Pity generates a sense of hopelessness; contrariwise, care produces a sense of empowerment. Care is aligned with the self-efficacy principles of awareness, well-being, responsibility, and student engagement.

CARE: COMMITMENT, ATTENTION, REFLECTION, AND EMPATHY

Educators, and I include myself, are do-gooders. Educators want to make the world a better place. If possible, educators want to save the world. With such laudable tendencies, educators must be certain not to choose the education profession as a means of feeling important and/or superior. They must guard against using this profession as a means of controlling something and/or somebody.

Educators must also guard against the desire to be the sage on stage in the same way they must examine their drum-major tendencies. The longings to be great, to be significant, and to be distinctive are not necessarily corrupt. For certain, each person should want to make his or her mark on humanity. However, such desires need to be flavored with the honey of care. The author further dissects the notion of care with the acronym CARE: commitment, attention, reflection, and empathy.

Commitment. One of the critical dispositions of an educator is commitment. It calls for a psychological attachment (Coladarci, 1992) and an extension into one's heart and soul (Noddings, 1992). When educators care, commitment is at the core of their pedagogical and administrative decisions (Gholami & Tirri, 2012). Committed educators also make students aware of, and prepare them for, the pursuit of viable postsecondary educational options regardless of family economic conditions or the lack of resourcefulness in their neighborhoods (Knight-Diop, 2010).

Caring teachers fill their classrooms with the warm sunlight of opportunity. Interestingly enough, both general efficacy (which reveals an external locus of control) and personal efficacy (which displays an internal locus of control) are strong predictors of commitment to teaching (Coladarci, 1992). In alignment with InTASC Standard #2 (learning differences) (CCSSO, 2013), caring teachers commit to serving students with individual learning, cultural, and community differences in the same way Mr. Feldman sought to see the assets of his student rather than her deficiencies.

Attention. According to Shevalier and McKenzie (2012), attention is the basis for genuine listening. Attention can be likened to emptying the content of one's soul in order to truly see what is inside the soul of another (Weil, 1977). Just as learners must give attention to the teacher and to the content, teachers must give attention to their students in order to experience the fundamental balance of teaching and learning.

In order to capture the attention of students enough to engage them, teachers must dedicate mental energy to students as individuals (Santrock, 2013). Hence, a committed educator is a thoughtful listener and a responsive observer (CCSSO, 2013). These characteristics are important so that the educator can get to know students well enough to identify their desires and to respond to their personal needs (Noddings, 2008; Noddings, 2002) as well as their cultural needs.

What is more, attention paves the way for relational knowing (Hollingsworth, 2001) which occurs when caring influences knowing. Mr. Feldman extended attentiveness toward Fay and, by extension, offered her individualized assistance simply because he was willing to develop his efficacy through the principle of care. In large measure, showing personalized, customized attention is another way to enhance educator efficacy. Such practices are in accordance with InTASC Standard #2 (CCSSO, 2013) that recommends giving attention to students' personal, family, and community experiences and norms.

Reflection. Since the early work of Dewey (1933), educators have been encouraged to be self-reflective so that they would not accept repeated, ineffective practices as status quo. In autobiographic self-studies, Gallavan and Webster-Smith (2012) unveiled that teachers must gain an understanding of themselves in relationship to others across multiple contexts, including their personal, professional, pedagogical, persuasive, public, political, and perplexed identities. One powerful outcome of requesting educators to reflect is that they gain rich opportunities to pinpoint the areas of their belief systems that unveil their inefficiencies and ineffectiveness in serving students (Webster-Smith, 2014). To be specific, Webster-Smith's (2014) Pyramid of Self-Reflection puts forth a model that inspires proactive and responsive reflection. Proactive reflection is intentional, purposeful, and deliberate forethought that is predictive and perceptive, while responsive reflection references the habitual afterthought and consideration of the outcomes of daily living. Accreditation standards also compel educators to engage in analysis and reflection to determine their impact on the learning environment they create (CCSSO, 2013). Overall, a consistent demonstration of care calls for a perpetual practice of reflection. Otherwise, they might yield to the temptation of stitching their cloak of low self-efficacy into a tailor-made suit of blame. Indeed, Mr. Feldman had the choices of blaming Fay's family for her plight, simply placing A's on her paper, and moving on with life. To the contrary, he chose to reflect upon how he might use this opportunity to enhance his self-efficacy with the values of care.

Empathy. Before touting the laurels of empathy, it is instructive to discuss the similarities and dissimilarities between sympathy and empathy. The most common similarities are that they both are emotive and are expressed as feelings. However, sympathy manifests as feelings of sorrow and pity. When a person feels sympathy, he does not necessarily understand the struggle, plight, or predicament of the other.

On the contrary, empathy heartens a person to take the journey with the other, much like Mr. Feldman's journey with Fay. To that end, Noddings (2002) encourages the carer to capture the affective state of the cared-for and O'Toole (1998) urges the carer to care for the other in tangible ways. Conscious caring is characterized by motivational displacement of the carer's own needs by those of the cared-for (Noddings, 1984). Showing empathy, then, enhances self-efficacy.

CONCLUSION

This chapter encourages educators to bolster their self-efficacy by enacting heartfelt and respectful caring relationships with students, families, and communities, without judgment. Caring educators collaborate with students to become dream makers rather than dream breakers. They facilitate learning in ways that help students to transition from their comfort zone to their courage zone. With appropriate manifestations of commitment, attention, reflection, and empathy, educators can surely enhance their self-efficacy.

QUESTIONS FOR EDUCATORS TO CONSIDER IN THEIR QUEST TO ENHANCE SELF-EFFICACY

Commitment:

1. How do I demonstrate my dedication to the bright future of the students that are entrusted to me?
2. How do I demonstrate devotion to the parents, guardians, or caregivers of my students?
3. Am I willing to endure the suffering that is inherent in developing human capacity?

Attention:

1. Do I idly watch the train wreck of student failure?
2. Do I attend to the needs of my students and make appropriate referrals to other teachers, administrators, counselors, and/or social workers to address the needs that are outside of my domain?
3. Do I know the difference between the needs I can address and those I cannot address?

Reflection:

1. Do I know what pure, natural, ethical, and authentic care looks/feels like in an educational setting?
2. How does my history of receiving care have an impact on my history of giving care?
3. Do I routinely examine my role in the behavior and achievement of students?

Empathy:

1. Do I exude warmth?
2. Do I attempt to walk in the shoes of my students by understanding their life's circumstances, by feeling their pain, and by preparing them to fulfill their dreams?
3. Do I treat my students as I would want my loved ones to be treated?

CARING TEACHER RESOURCES

A Quality Teacher Is a Caring Teacher. http://www.nea.org/tools/15751.htm.
Four Ways Teachers Can Show They Care. http://greatergood.berkeley.edu/article/item/caring_teacher_student_relationship.
Nice Is Not Enough. http://academics.holycross.edu/files/Article.pdf.

Teachers Care. http://teach.com/what/teachers-care.
Teachers Who Put the "A" in Caring. http://www.gallup.com/poll/6049/teachers-who-put-a-caring.aspx.

REFERENCES

Antrop-Gonzalez, R., & De Jesus, A. (2006). Toward a theory of critical care in urban small school reform: Examining structures and pedagogies of caring in two Latino-community based schools. *International Journal of Qualitative Studies in Education, 19*, 409–33.

Bandura, A. (1977). Self-efficacy: Toward a unifying theory of behavior change. *Psychological Review, 84*, 191–215.

Coladarci, T. (1992, Summer). Teachers' sense of efficacy and commitment to teaching. *The Journal of Experimental Education, 60*(4), 323–37.

Council of Chief State School Officers (CCSSO). (2013, April). *InTASC model core teaching standards and learning progressions for teachers 1.0: A resource for ongoing teacher development.* Washington, DC: Author.

Council of Chief State School Officers (CCSSO). (2008). *Educational leadership policy s tandards: ISLLC 2008.* Washington, DC: Author.

Dewey, J. (1933). *Democracy and education.* New York, NY: Free Press.

Gallavan, N., & Webster-Smith, A. (2012). Cultural competence and the recursive nature of conscientization. In C. J. Craig, and N. P. Gallavan (Eds.), *Teacher Education Yearbook XXI (Part 1). Issues in education: Examining the perspectives of student candidates, teachers, and teacher educators* (pp. 401–19). Hershey, PA: Taylor and Francis.

Gholami, K., & Tirri, K. (2012). Caring teaching as a moral practice: An exploratory study on perceived dimensions of caring teaching. *Education Research International* 2012, Article ID 954274, http://dx.doi.org/10.1155/2012/954274.

Goldstein, L. S., & Lake, V. E. (2000). Love, love, and more love for children: Exploring preservice teachers' understandings of caring. *Teaching and Teacher Education, 16*(8), 861–72.

Gordon, S., Benner, P., & Noddings, N. (Eds.). (1996). *Caregiving: Readings in knowledge, practice, ethics, and politics.* Philadelphia, PA: University of Pennsylvania Press.

Hansen, D. T. (1998). The moral is in the practice. *Teaching and Teacher Education, 14*(6), 643–55.

Hollingsworth, S. (2001). Relational knowing in the reform of educational cultures. *Teachers College Record, 103*(2), 240–66.

Husu, J., & Tirri, K. (2012). Developing whole school pedagogical values: A case of going through the ethos of "good schooling.." *Teaching and Teacher Education, 23*(4) 390–401.

Isenbarger, L., & Zembylas, M. (2006). The emotional labour of caring in teaching. *Teaching and Teacher Education, 22*(1), 120–34.

Knight-Diop, M. (2010). Closing the gap: Enacting care and facilitating Black students' educational access in the creation of a high school college-going culture. *Journal of Education for Students Placed at Risk, 15*(1–2), 158–172.

Noddings, N. (2007). Caring as relation and virtue in teaching. In P. S. Ivanhoe, and R. Walker (Eds.), *Working virtue: Virtue ethics and contemporary moral problems* (pp. 41–60). Oxford: Oxford University Press.

Noddings, N. (2002). *Starting at home: Caring and social policy.* Berkeley, CA: University of California Press.

Noddings, N. (1999). Two concepts of caring. *Philosophy of Education.* Retrieved from http://www.ed.uiuc.edu/EPS/PES-yearbook/1999/Noddingss.asp.

Noddings, N. (1992). *The challenge to care in schools: An alternative approach to education.* New York, NY: Teachers College Press.

Noddings, N. (1984). *Caring: A feminine approach to ethics and moral education.* Berkeley, CA: University of California Press.

O'Toole, K. (1998) Noddings: To know what matters to you, observe your actions. Retrieved from *Stanford Online Report,* http://news-service.stanford.edu/news/1998/february4/ Noddingss.html.

Santrock, J. W. (2013). *Adolescence* (15th ed.). New York, NY: McGraw-Hill Higher Education.

Shevalier, R., and McKenzie, B. A. (2012, November). Culturally responsive teaching as an ethics- and care-based approach to urban education. *Urban Education, 47(6),* 1086–1105.

Siddle Walker, V. (1996a). Interpersonal caring in the "good" segregated schooling of African-American children. In D. Esker-Rich, and J. A. Van Galen (Eds.), *Caring in an Unjust World* (pp. 129–46). New York: SUNY Press.

Siddle Walker, V. (1996b). *Their highest potential.* Chapel Hill, NC: University of North Carolina Press.

Webster-Smith, A. (2014). Scaling the pyramid of self-reflection: A model for teachers to contest demographic destiny. In E. Pultorak (Ed.), *Reflectivity and cultivating student learning: Critical elements for enhancing a global community of learners and educators.* (pp. 29-52). Lanham, MD: Rowman and Littlefield.

Weil, S. (1977). *Simone Weil reader.* G. A. Panichas (Ed.). New York, NY: McKaye.

Chapter Three

Expanding from Self to Collective Classroom Efficacy

A Tale of Two Classroom Communities

LeAnn G. Putney, Suzanne H. Jones, and Brett D. Campbell

Case One: The first day of school in my first year of teaching, and I feel emotionally and mentally prepared to begin our journey of learning. Prior to the beginning of school, I devoted careful thought and planning on fostering a sense of community with these students. My planning included academic lessons, community building activities and a classroom with blank bulletin boards for students to share about themselves and to provide evidence of what they were learning. Yet, I still wonder how will I bring together a new group of students from working class families, refugees and immigrants, with seven different languages spoken in the classroom?

This scenario is not terribly different from other new teacher experiences, and similar to some situations faced by experienced teachers who have faced rezoning efforts in cities following expansive growth resulting in new schools cropping up to be filled with excited students and teachers. The first day of school can be quite intimidating. As one of the students from this teacher's class stated, "I was scared the first part of the year. . . . I remember a lot of people trying to take over, like being the boss, trying to take charge of the group" (Marc, personal communication).

Case Two: Ms. Falls, in speaking to the fourth-grade class from next door who will be her fifth-grade incoming class: "Ok. So it is nice to meet you. You have come into a room that is, what we would like to consider, to be a kid-operated classroom. That means the activities and the work in here really generates from the students. You are going to see a sample of what we do

25

today. You are going to hear about various things we do and how we do it. You are going to hear students not the teacher. The only time you are going to hear me is this morning.

"We also know that your class has been very challenged doing some of the things you had to do this year, like walk in the hallways, stay on task during learning activities, relate to each other in your classroom, or relate as a class when you go to a special. Next year, we hope you will turn around and do things differently. Not only do we hope, but you are expected to turn around and do it differently."

This experienced teacher had expressed concern for her upcoming year because she understood the reputation of the incoming class. She knew she would have to work closely with this group to help them break out of their prior behavioral patterns. The way she went about it was to enlist the help of her current classroom community to enact a "Network for Learning Conference" so that the fifth-grade citizens could demonstrate to the fourth graders how to be successful learners in this classroom.

Our intent with this chapter is to make visible the efforts put forward by two classroom teachers in different school settings to ensure an efficacious classroom environment. Such an environment is often referred to as a "learning community" or "positive classroom climate," but we named this construct "Collective Classroom Efficacy" (CCE). The distinction is the focus on building academics and social life skills to ensure both scholarship and stewardship in the classroom and in preparation for life beyond school. We take you along on the journey to better understand this construct and to recognize how to construct it for yourself in your classroom.

THEORETICAL FRAMEWORK

A rich body of literature concerning collective efficacy to date focuses on school-wide efficacy and teacher efficacy, which relates to beliefs that shape teachers' judgments about their capabilities in promoting student learning (Goddard, Hoy, & Hoy, 2004). The emphasis of that research has been to identify characteristics and resulting effects of teachers and schools with high levels of collective efficacy. One gap in this corpus of research is that of collective efficacy at the classroom level.

Our prior research (Putney and Broughton, 2011) examined CCE as a construct that is socially constructed and developed over time by classroom participants. Through this construct, the classroom teacher as classroom community organizer (Bandura, 1997) promotes an interdependence and dialogic interplay among students that results in a shared sense of ability to achieve personal and common academic goals.

In his study of Vygotsky's work, Bandura (1993) noted, "Children's intellectual development cannot be isolated from the social relations within which it is embedded and from its interpersonal effects" (p. 120). As we were interested in *how* classroom teachers could foster efficacy across a group of students, we needed to use an explanatory theory that illustrated development of individuals and a collective over time in a cultural setting. Using a sociocultural perspective (Palincsar, 1998; Vygotsky, 1978; 1986) allowed us to examine the participants' lived experiences as resources for academic success.

Our findings helped us understand the role of the classroom teacher in facilitating CCE, which exemplifies InTASC Standard #3, "The teacher works with others to create environments that support individual and collaborative learning, and that encourage positive social interaction, active engagement in learning, and self-motivation" (CCSSO, 2011). Understanding this InTASC standard as applied to real-life teaching situations is instrumental in making standards relevant for teachers.

We have recognized in our research with classroom teachers that the approach to constructing a classroom environment conducive to producing CCE is individually tailored by the classroom teacher each year in accordance with the classroom culture being created through the interactions with and among students. At the same time, certain principles of practice can be considered and highlighted in our work so that pre-service, novice, and sometimes even well-practiced teachers can better appreciate how to approach their classroom structure to lay the groundwork for constructing a strong and productive learning environment.

Constructing Collective Classroom Efficacy

Our approach to understanding the classrooms represented by the two cases is that of viewing classrooms acting as local cultures (Tuyay et al., 1995; Putney & Frank, 2008). This perspective presumes that classroom participants construct and reconstruct patterned ways of being and interacting together. In addition, the norms and language produced in these classrooms become local resources for all participants to extend and facilitate learning.

Thus, novice teachers may find a challenge in bringing together a diverse group of students into a cohesive cultural unit because they are working with differing beliefs systems and cultures and, potentially, even different language usage. Given that each classroom collective creates a particular culture, even seasoned teachers may encounter a group of students who resist entry into the common cultural experience, who do not engender a sense of collective efficacy, and who are even resistant to constructing it from the beginning of the school year.

For purposes of illustration, we are juxtaposing two classroom scenarios—the first being the vignette we highlighted in the beginning, the second being an experienced fifth-grade classroom teacher. The cross-case comparison is to demonstrate that engaging students in a strong classroom community can be challenging for all teachers. We also intend to show in what ways teachers can organize their classrooms to best promote a classroom culture of students exhibiting strong "positive social interaction, active engagement in learning, and high levels of self-motivation" (CCSSO, 2011).

METHOD

This study used a qualitative cross-case comparison of two diverse classrooms. For purposes of this study, we examined data from field notes, interviews, and teacher reflections related to the role of community organizer uncovered in a prior study. In each case, the teacher acted as community organizer and worked toward producing a cohesive classroom community. We selected the two cases to illustrate how different teachers can establish similar principles of classroom practice, even though their experiences differ. We also intended the outcomes of the cases to provide insight in terms of preparing students to work productively as resources for each other.

We began our study with Case One (Ms. Broughton) to examine the construct of CCE following a first-year teacher interacting with a group of sixth-grade students who had come together in a new school setting. The classroom teacher in Case Two (Ms. Falls) is an experienced teacher, known for her expertise in constructing cohesive communities, who had to overcome the resistant nature of a group of students in order to engage in student-centered community building. Juxtaposing both cases allows for extracting the principles of practice that CCE holds for classrooms teachers to be community organizers in their classrooms.

In addition, the use of cross-case analysis between the two different cases provided us with a rich point (Agar, 1994) for the purpose of teasing out the principles of practice related to building a classroom culture and framing instruction (Table 3.1) that the teachers implemented as classroom community organizers and actuators (Wink and Putney, 2002). In this way, we could make visible how to begin to establish the classroom environment that supports, fosters, and nurtures CCE.

Case One. The elementary teacher for this case worked with sixth-grade students ($n = 21$) in an inner city Title 1 school located in the western United States. This was her first year of teaching. The school population was ethnically and linguistically diverse; 83 percent of the students received free or reduced lunch. This was the first year of the elementary school, as it was built due to a rezoning process. Therefore, all of the students were new to the school and placed in a situation of having to make new acquaintances as they were brought together from other schools.

The data consisted of teacher reflections, interview data, and analysis of classroom artifacts that included teacher plans, student end-of-year reflections, and student-generated poetry. The focus of the data analysis was on the organizational efforts of both teachers at the beginning of school, and then adaptations made by the teachers to the classroom community structure over time.

Case Two. The fifth-grade teacher in this case was in her sixth year of teaching but in her second year at this particular school. The school was highly diverse, located on an urban university campus, with 85 percent of students receiving free or reduced lunch. Ms. Falls had been selected for the study as an exemplar of someone constructing an academically strong and socially responsible fifth-grade classroom community. The school principal had purposely assigned this group to Ms. Falls as she had already proven her expertise with prior challenging students.

When the students in Case Two were fourth graders, they had developed a negative reputation within the school, promoting themselves as the "baddest class in the school." It was Ms. Falls's challenge to develop "positive social interaction, active engagement in learning, and high levels of self-motivation" in this group of students (CCSSO, 2011). The anticipated clash between this teacher's student-centered governance and a fairly resistant group of incoming fifth graders provided for a unique exploration of CCE.

RESULTS

From the first days of school, both teachers began to work with the students to establish norms and expectations for academic success. For Ms. Broughton, the challenge was to bring together students who did not know each other and help them recognize their similarities while valuing their diversity. The challenge for Ms. Falls was quite the opposite, in the sense that these incoming fifth graders had already formed a less than positive cohesive bond the prior year. In what follows, we illustrate the common classroom themes of constructing classroom culture and framing instruction for fostering Collective Classroom Efficacy (Table 3.1).

Constructing Classroom Culture

Case One. In the days preceding the first day of school, Ms. Broughton constructed a "Big Friendly Grid" (BFG) (Sapon-Shevin, 1998), a large chart that listed each student's name across the top of the chart as well as horizontally down the first row of the chart. The purpose of the BFG was to help students get to know one another by finding things they had in common.

Table 3.1.   Establishing CCE from first weeks of school

	CASE 1	CASE 2
Teacher	1st year of teaching; newly rezoned school	6th year of teaching; 2nd year at this school
Student Issues	Student's first year at new school—	"Baddest Class" from prior year
Constructing Classroom Culture	Community Circle to enhance cohesiveness Big Friendly Grid (BFG) (Sapon-Shevin, 1998)	Executive Council for self-governance Created Network For Learning Conference
Framing Instruction	TRIBES (Gibbs, 2001) Minds-on/hands-on activities and reflection	Kovalic's LifeSkills (1994) Inquiry process, scaffolding learning

Students were given twenty minutes on the first day of school to visit with one another in order to find something they each had in common. The students would then find their corresponding names and matching box on the grid and write their commonality in that box.

For example, Angelica and Elisha both liked playing 4-square during recess. Angela would find her name on the top row of the BFG while Elisha found her name on the first column of the chart. Then, where their name rows coincided, they wrote "4-square" in the box. Students enthusiastically worked together throughout the first three weeks of school to complete the BFG. It was common to find students talking with each other about their commonalities during learning activities, as well as while they were at recess or lunch.

Also, Ms. Broughton and the students co-constructed their list of classroom rules. A Community Circle was convened that involved everyone sharing what rules they thought would help to create a positive and respectful classroom community. The ideas were grouped into similar categories and vetted down to a set of rules everyone agreed upon and believed they could enact. The students wrote the rules on a large chart, and each student signed their name as a way of showing agreement and ownership in the rules. This sense of self-governance was an important component of these students achieving a sense of collective classroom efficacy.

Ms. Broughton used daily Community Circles as a place for students to share how they were feeling that day, to discuss the day's agenda, for students to share appreciations for peers, and to talk about any issues related to how well they were working together as a community. Sometimes students would convey their concerns anonymously by writing them on a small piece of paper and placing it in the Community Circle box. The rules for Community Circle were that students were expected to be respectful toward one another. Students showed respect through listening, sharing, and holding the belief that they were all in this together.

Case Two. Ms. Falls framed the classroom each year as a model of the community they lived in. Within this community, individuals would take on different roles mirroring those of the larger community. These roles would reflect government roles; a mayor, a lieutenant mayor, an executive council, and individuals with policing responsibilities. The classroom community each year would begin by developing their own norms, or rules.

These norms were jointly constructed in the first three weeks of school, and they modeled some of the life skills from Kovalik and Olsen's model (1994). The focus of a self-regulated community was not on reprimanding one another but on encouraging positive classroom behavior and acknowledging such positive behavior. The expectation of the teacher for herself was as a co-participant and community organizer, while still retaining the right to interject her authority as needed.

As mentioned earlier, Ms. Falls was informed toward the end of the year that she would be "inheriting" members of the fourth-grade class from the teacher next door. The entire school was acutely aware that this group was self-proclaimed as the "baddest class" in the school. In consultation with the university researcher in her classroom, she devised a Network for Learning Conference (cf. Putney, 2007).

The idea was for the current class of fifth graders to apprentice the incoming students into the classroom culture via a daylong conference format. They would present to the fourth graders the governance structure and how they jointly constructed and reviewed their classroom norms, followed by group activities related to the various content areas. In this way, she hoped to start the new academic year with the students buying into the norms and expectations co-constructed from the prior year.

From the first day of class, students worked toward getting to know one another, and they began constructing their norms as "ways of working together." They reviewed the norms from the prior class that they had been introduced to as fourth graders during the Network for Learning Conference. While the students did construct the norms together, they did not take up the norms until the second semester of the school year. Ms. Falls, using her own positive persistence, continued to scaffold the students into the personal and interpersonal responsibility structure by holding the students accountable to their norms.

Academically, the teacher expected all her students to master the content. Behavioral expectations were laid out that said that students not only needed to regulate their own behavior, but as a classroom community, they also needed to assist their peers in regulating their behavior as well. Community expectations followed this same line of thinking, resulting in personal and academic responsibility. Knowing that this group might not have been as willing to work toward productive behavior, Ms. Falls introduced the idea of a peer court. The students became so successful at arbitrating their own behaviors that they were asked to conduct peer court for other classes in the school as well.

FRAMING INSTRUCTION

Case One. Ms. Broughton used two central strategies for framing learning activities. First, lessons were typically developed using the Tribes (Gibbons, 2006) format. This included the following: 1) Set learning objectives and behavior expectations, 2) students engage in minds-on/hands-on activities, 3) reflection (academic, social, individual), and 4) share appreciations with team members. In this way, academic content was integrated with social building skills throughout the day. It is with this approach to instruction that collective classroom efficacy had the opportunity to develop throughout the school year.

Second, students were assigned to small groups, consisting of four students. What is important to note is that the student groups changed throughout the day, depending upon the content area studied. For example, a group of four students would work together for mathematics, but then would be in a different group for literacy, and even a different group for science. The aim of rotating students in various groups throughout the day was to encourage all students to get to know one another, provide peer-tutoring opportunities, and enact the class motto "We are all in this together."

As noted by Muharem, one of the students, at the end of the year, "We bonded so well together that it felt like when somebody succeeded, you did something right. Because we were working with each other and teaching each other. Because all of us did share so much of ourselves in our groups." From the end-of-year reflections, Carlos stated, "It was the best! We all came together. We were like family," while Marc explained, "Sixth grade, it took a while to get used to each other but after we did, we were pretty much like family."

Case Two. Ms. Falls framed her instruction around inquiry-based practices, and she first modeled the type of interactions she expected students to produce, whether in constructing and reviewing norms or in discussing their readings or reviewing math and science problems. She provided support and gradually turned over more and more responsibility to students until proficiency levels necessary to accomplish the activities independently were evident. Her work with students in their literary clubs provides an example of how they worked together.

Ms. Falls would group students into literary clubs, based on the different levels of readers and thematic novels that were used in the classroom. Early in the year, she modeled the metacognitive skills needed to discriminate important story elements, such as setting, main characters, plot, theme, climax, author's purpose, and real-world connections. Students were allowed to practice identifying these elements before they were expected to do them independently.

As they moved through their literary clubs, students applied the conventional concepts and skills of reading and interpreting literature, such as predicting, retelling, interpreting, judging, analyzing, and synthesizing. Students actively listened and came to understand how to identify a common theme across various literary works, appraise and use illustrations, recognize genres, and discuss and comprehend various writing styles of authors. They also learned how to link their literary experiences with real-world experiences.

DISCUSSION AND CONCLUSION

Often students develop beliefs about their class as a group. They may differ in cohesiveness, degree of self-regulation, and perception of academic ability as a group. Those perceptions about themselves as a group will develop with or without teacher input and guidance. We selected two teachers who conscientiously strove to develop a positive classroom community. The reason for this goal was different for each teacher. The first teacher established a community goal as a reaction to students being assigned to a new school as a result of rezoning, and the second, to form a highly cohesive group of students who needed redirection.

The process also was different in how the culture was identified by students and their teacher through the activities and roles assumed. The first case built on commonalities and collaborative learning concurrently. In the second case, the teacher used existing cohesiveness to build self-governance and collaborative learning activities. Through both processes, each community reported greater cohesiveness and more positive images of themselves individually and collectively as learners.

One commonality was that the teachers saw themselves, and were perceived by students, as members of the classroom community. The teachers assumed certain roles to achieve the goals they had for their students. This sense of membership contributed to CCE. Historically, elementary school teachers have been expected to improve academic achievement and provide socialization for their students. We found in these two cases that both goals, academic achievement and socialization, were not treated as independent areas; rather they were reciprocal influences.

We propose moving beyond InTASC Standard 3(b), which focuses only on collaborative-learning experiences. Collaborative learning often consists of short-term activities (Palinscar & Brown, 1984; Artz & Armour-Thomas,

1992). In both cases, the teachers engaged students in collaborative activities, while also challenging them to become self-directed learners. Through goal setting and reflection, learners were able to monitor progress toward academic growth. In these two cases, collaboration was ongoing and across all domains of classroom activities: academics, classroom management, community engagement, and socialization.

Early in the conceptualization of self-efficacy for teaching, a distinction was made between general efficacy, which includes factors in learning beyond a teacher's control (such as student's home life), and personal efficacy, which reflects the teacher's personal factors (Bandura, 1997; Tschannen-Moran & Woolfolk Hoy, 2001). Both are key components to be considered when building a classroom community.

We conceptualized CCE as including both general and personal factors and also including perceptions of both teachers and students. In treating learning as a community goal, one community member's shortcoming is another member's strength. This sense of community, in these two cases, eliminates those aspects often seen as negative. Both teachers guided this sense of community and hence CCE, through the social and instructional activities.

DISCUSSION QUESTIONS

1. How am I integrating interpersonal relationship development into academic activities?
2. How might I organize student groups so that everyone has opportunities to share expertise throughout each day? (Am I grouping students so that one who struggles with reading, but is strong in math, has the opportunity to peer teach in math and be peer taught in reading?)
3. Am I keeping student groups dynamic throughout the day, having students work with different peers in reading, math, science, and so forth, such that everyone has opportunities:

   of teaching and being taught;

   of helping one another succeed with the learning activity;

   of getting to know one another as they work in groups?

These questions are especially important for those students who likely wouldn't interact with one another in typical social and academic settings.

RESOURCES

Tribes Learning Community. http://tribes.com/.
Kagan Cooperative Learning Strategies. http://www.kaganonline.com/catalog/cooperative_learning.php.

Microsociety. http://www.microsociety.org.
Edutopia. http://www.edutopia.org/.
Kovalic, S. http://www.thecenter4learning.com/html/resources/lifeskills.htm.

REFERENCES

Agar, M. (1994). *Language shock: Understanding the culture of conversation.* New York, NY: William Morrow and Company.

Artz, A. F., & Armour-Thomas, E. (1992). Development of a cognitive-metacognitive framework for protocol analysis of mathematical problem solving. *Cognition and Instruction, 9,* 137–75.

Bandura, A. (1993). Perceived self-efficacy in cognitive development and functioning. *Educational Psychologist, 28,* 117–48.

Bandura, A. (1997). *Self-efficacy: The exercise of control.* New York, NY: W. H. Freeman & Company.

Council of Chief State School Officers (CCSSO). (2011). *Interstate teacher assessment and support consortium (InTASC) model core teaching standards: A resource for state dialogue.* Washington, DC: CCSSO. Retrieved from http://www.ccsso.org/documents/2011/intasc_model_core_teaching_standards_2011.pdf.

Gibbs, J. (2001). *TRIBES: A new way of learning and being together.* Windsor, CA: CenterSource Systems.

Goodard, R. S., Hoy, W. K., & Hoy, A. W. (2004). Collective efficacy beliefs: Theoretical developments, empirical evidence, and future directions. *Educational Researcher, 33*(3), 3–13.

Kovalik, S., & Olsen, K. (1994). *ITI, the model: Integrated thematic instruction* (3rd ed.). Kent, WA: Books for Educators.

Palincsar, A. S. (1998). Social constructivist perspectives on teaching and learning. *Annual Review of Psychology, 49*(1), 345–75.

Palincsar, A. S., & Brown, A. L. (1984). Reciprocal teaching of comprehension-fostering and comprehension-monitoring activities. *Cognition and Instruction, 1*(2), 117–75.

Putney, L. G. (2007). Discursive practices as cultural resources: Formulating identities for individual and collective in an inclusive classroom setting. *International Journal of Educational Research, 46*(3–4), 129–40.

Putney, L. G., & Broughton, S. H. (2011). Collective classroom efficacy: The teacher's role as community organizer. *Journal of Teacher Education, 62*(1), 93–105.

Putney, L. G., & Frank, C. R. (2008). Looking through ethnographic eyes at classrooms acting as cultures. *Ethnography and Education, 3*(2), 211–28.

Sapon-Shevin, M. (1998). *Because we can change the world: A practice guide to building cooperative, inclusive classroom communities.* Boston, MA: Pearson Education.

Tschannen-Moran, M. & Woolfolk Hoy, A. (2001). Teacher efficacy: Capturing an elusive construct. *Teaching and Teacher Education, 17,* 783–805.

Tuyay, S., Floriani, A., Yeager, B., Dixon, C., & Green, J. (1995). Constructing an integrated, inquiry-oriented approach in classrooms: A cross-case analysis of social, literate, and academic practice. *Journal of Classroom Interaction, 30* (2), 1–15.

Vygotsky, L. S. (1978). *Mind in society: The development of higher psychological processes.* Cambridge, MA: Harvard University Press.

Vygotsky, L. S. (1986). *Thought and language.* Cambridge, MA: MIT Press.

Chapter Four

Advancing Self-Efficacy with Academic, Pedagogical, Assessment, and Learner Content

Nancy P. Gallavan

Madison is an aspiring teacher candidate who wants to teach grades five to eight. From volunteer work at the community center, Madison believes she connects well with middle-level learners; she predicts she will acquire effective pedagogical knowledge and skills to build upon her academic content knowledge and skills.

A hardworking college student earning an average grade point, Madison passes the general education exam by only a few points, allowing her to enter the teacher-preparation program. She is surprised at the difficulty of the exam yet accepts that she needs to dedicate herself to her studies. She wants to be an outstanding teacher and realizes that passing the upcoming exams poses some serious career challenges.

During the introductory course, Madison visits a school conducting her first clinical field experience focused on content. There she realizes that she is not "as smart" as most of the teachers and some of the students. She cannot readily recall the content knowledge and skills being taught in the lessons. This insight alarms her; Madison hopes that the teachers' guides that accompany the students' textbooks will provide her with the information she needs to teach her own future students.

During subsequent clinical field experiences, Madison begins to comprehend the importance of the teachers' expertise with the motivation, implementation, environment, and negotiation (MIEN) of the curriculum, instruction, assessments, and learner content.

With discursive awareness leading to critical consciousness (Gallavan Critical Consciousness Model found in Gallavan and Webster-Smith, 2012),

37

Madison recognizes the professional composure modeled by the teacher, who seamlessly scaffolds upon learners' current knowledge and skills to capture their attention, engage them in activities, pace the learning, and make the objectives meaningful. Madison carefully notes that without linking the purpose and procedures to both the learning and individual learner, the lessons would not be successful or satisfying for either the teacher or the learners.

Madison's newly awakened attention to the depth, breadth, accountability, and context of content requisite for effective teaching and learning is reinforced. She agonizes over her comprehension of content, wonders about her abilities to stay apprised of new information as well as to advance her current knowledge and skills, and hopes that she gains tools and techniques for communicating and connecting content with her future middle-level learners and their lives.

Madison talks with her cousin Abby, a fourth-grade teacher starting her sixth year of teaching. Abby reassures Madison that all new teachers are afraid they will not know the subject matter and will not be able to reach all learners. Easing her discomfort, Abby tells Madison that most new teachers do not feel ready for their classrooms and learners. Abby continues by showing Madison her effective routines based on her own education and experiences supplemented by her colleagues' guidance and support.

MADISON'S CONCERNS ABOUT CONTENT

Madison's encounters portray a common situation for many teacher candidates: becoming a successful and satisfied teacher requires demonstrating proficiency with academic, pedagogical, assessment, and learner content. Presuming she will learn about content in her teacher-preparation program, Madison also intends to gain insights from career teachers like her cousin. However, Madison has discovered that at times the advice she receives from her cousin does not match the recommendations she gleans from her university instructors and courses.

Madison is not alone; many candidates are not highly proficient with content. Candidates express doubts about their capabilities and are unsure of the mismatched guidance they receive with their content knowledge and skills. Feistritzer (2010), found that only 44 percent of all new teachers reported that they felt "very competent" to teach their content subject areas. Remarkably, 2 percent reported that they felt "not very competent," and 1 percent reported that they felt "not at all competent." Teachers gain competence with content only through professional guidance and accumulated experience teaching their subject matter.

Not only should candidates and teachers demonstrate comprehension of their academic content subject area in isolation, but they must also be proficient in their abilities to incorporate their content with content within their field of study, integrate their content with all other content, assess progress (of teaching and learning), and connect the content to their learners' contemporary needs and interests.

However, researchers have determined that 77 percent of all teacher-education college graduates graduate in the lower two-thirds of their graduating classes (Auguste, Kihn, & Miller, 2010). This statistic indicates that most candidates do not earn high grade point averages, and, most likely, they do not excel in their general education courses, as teacher candidates tend to earn higher grade point averages in their education courses (Koedel, 2011).

Thus, new teachers are more likely to not possess the desired fluency with their academic content beneficial to increasing their learners' achievements, to help their learners make new connections integrating content across the curriculum and into their communities, and to challenge their learners' thinking. Compounding this situation, only 14 percent of the teachers working with at-risk learner populations graduated in the upper one-third of their graduating classes (Auguste, Kihn, & Miller, 2010). Thus, a disproportionate percentage of teachers earning lower grade point averages work with learners who need the most assistance.

Teacher effectiveness is the primary influence on learner achievement (The Wallace Foundation, 2008). Learners who are taught by highly effective teachers three years in a row score as much as 50 percentile points higher on achievement measures than learners who are taught by ineffective teachers for three years in a row (National Commission on Teaching and America's Future [NCTAF], 2010). Therefore, becoming an effective teacher is essential for each learner, teacher, and school and for society.

TODAY'S TEACHER CANDIDATES

In general, today's teacher candidates tend to be the first college graduates in their families; they come from families with less education and bring fewer travel experiences for them to reference as part of their amassed intellectual inventories (Gallavan, 2007). Exacerbating this situation, many teacher candidates attend institutions fairly close to their homes and hope to be offered teaching positions in the same vicinity (Feistritzer, 2010). Since teacher preparation is readily available on most university campuses and less expensive at state-supported institutions, today's candidates tend to select their universities based on cost and convenience, rather than programs and opportunities.

Approximately 13 percent of college graduates earn degrees in teacher preparation (United States Census Bureau, 2012), and frequently teacher preparation courses are viewed as being easier (Arum and Roska, 2010). Adjunct instructors in the teacher-preparation program may be the same classroom teachers who taught the candidates as P–12 learners in the area schools.

Moreover, since 2005, 33 percent of all new teachers enter the profession through alternative preparation programs not held on college campuses (Feistritzer, 2010). Therefore, candidates may not interact with other university students and/or teacher candidates; candidates may be taught by adjunct instructors who are new to and/or void of the education and experience of most university teacher educators.

Researchers report that only 27 percent of all university instructors are full-time tenure-track professional teacher educators (American Federation of Teachers, 2010). The trend for hiring more clinical or adjunct instructors means that candidates may not be provided the most current and valuable research relevant to academic, pedagogical, assessment, or learner content. Clinical and adjunct instructors may not be as committed to and well informed about the university educational programs; likewise, clinical and adjunct instructors may not be as available and supportive of candidates' understanding and development.

Researchers also reveal that 50 percent of all candidates enrolled in their clinical experiences are unsupervised (Levine, 2006). Teacher candidates and new teachers report that they learn more about teaching in the classroom from their colleagues than they learn in their teacher preparation.

Across the United States, 26 percent of the teaching force has fewer than ten years of experience (Feistritzer, 2010), and although 52 percent of all teachers have earned advanced degrees, researchers also find that advanced degrees seem to make no difference in learner achievement (Clotfelter, Ladd, and Vigdor, 2010). Therefore, candidates and teachers may be limited in their content knowledge and skills due to their backgrounds as well as their instructors and supervision.

Although annual professional development is required of most teachers throughout their careers, continuing education workshops appear to improve the teaching strategies and learners' achievements for only the first five years of teachers' careers (Aaronson, Barrow, & Sander, 2007). Researchers show that only 45 percent of teachers view professional development as contributing positively to their content competence (Feistritzer, 2010).

Teachers report that they learn best from experienced teachers; however, experienced teachers comprise merely 50 percent of all teachers, and that percentage continues to decline due to age-related retirement and job dissatisfaction (NCTAF, 2010). Teachers report that the current emphasis in classrooms is focused on learner achievement and performance-based assessments; more accountability and paperwork are required of teachers to demonstrate the progress of every learner. Perhaps challenges with content without professional guidance and support accelerate teacher attrition.

TEACHER SELF-EFFICACY

Bandura (1977) defines self-efficacy as "beliefs in one's capabilities to organize and execute the courses of action required to produce given attainments" (p. 3). Rinaldo et al. (2009) emphasize that teachers must engage in critical self-assessment (Ross & Bruce, 2007) of their self-efficacy, reflecting (Schön, 1983) upon their learner intent with academic and pedagogical (Shulman, 1987) assessment (Black et al., 2004), and learner (Davies and Osguthorpe, 2003) content. Ultimately, assessing and analyzing the teaching in relationship to learner intent advances the conversations and characteristics associated with teacher self-efficacy.

Learner intent enables candidates and teachers to advance their understanding of the learning process and goals of enhancing self-efficacy. The three perspectives (Shulman, 1987) include (1) habitual intent: predetermining the outcome and using reflection as a means of description, explanation, and justification; (2) situational intent: participating in continuous reflection that changes direction based on the context but may not be long lasting; (3) worthy intent: engaging in continuous reflection that changes directions based on concepts and tends to be long lasting.

Introducing and modeling these symbiotic experiences with candidates during their teacher preparation equips and empowers candidates to incorporate them to enhance their own self-efficacy and to use with their future learners.

Academic Content

Every academic discipline associated with P–12 schooling is founded on the principles and practices within a particular field of study. This body of information includes knowledge, skills, and dispositions comprising an ever-expanding reservoir of theories and research, vocabulary and concepts, purposes and possibilities. Academic content may be labeled "what to teach and learn." Many different professions and products are associated with the study and applications of each academic discipline, manifested in seemingly unlimited expressions visible across the interdependent global society.

All academic disciplines continue to grow and change with advancements in research and practices over time. Thus, content is not confined to a finite, static set. To stay current with content and still contain the content, policy makers and professional educators persist in their endeavors to establish a frame of academic standards and expectations to guide teaching and learning for P–12 schools. However, challenges arise when the published frame is interpreted as both the requirements and the limitations. If the frame includes sample items illustrative of the standard, then many educators replace the standard with the samples.

Academic content encompasses much more than a frame and samples; candidates and teachers must be prepared with the entire body of knowledge, skills, and dispositions related to their academic subject area. Content courses designed to support a teacher's learning process are one of the most valuable ways to increase levels of self-efficacy (Swackhamer et al., 2009). As candidates and teachers enhance their self-efficacy, they tend to become more proficient with academic content. The academic content can be thought of as the "what to teach."

Pedagogical Content

Self-efficacy includes the belief that one has both the capacity and the will to demonstrate the capacity to do what is right and good because it is right and good (Gallavan, 2011). Therefore, teachers must assess their proficiencies honestly and construct learning experiences holistically to increase their learners' knowledge, skills, and dispositions naturally and authentically. Pedagogical content embodies information necessary for curricular development. Teachers may think of pedagogical content as "how to teach and learn."

Shulman (1986, 1987, 1992) created the Model of Pedagogical Reasoning, which identifies six components in a continuous cycle: comprehension, transformation, instruction, evaluation, reflection, and new comprehension. The six components of Shulman's Model of Pedagogical Reasoning guide and support candidates and teachers as they advance their efficacy and professionalism. Once teachers engage in reflection and reconstruction, they are becoming highly efficacious.

Czernaik (1990) found that highly efficacious teachers were more likely to use learner-centered approaches such as inquiry-, project-, and service-learning-based collaborative experiences. Teachers with low levels of self-efficacy tend to use more teacher-directed methods such as lecturing, note taking, and textbook reading.

Becoming highly efficacious means starting with the anticipated outcome known as the "end" or "assessment" and working backwards by selecting the appropriate instruction and aligning it with the identified content that makes the standards inviting and exciting for a particular group of learners. The learning process should be holistic, so academic and pedagogical content are selected to provide honest information coupled with authentic activities culminating in natural outcomes or ends (that link to future learning).

The Backward Assessment Model (BAM) (Wiggins and McTighe, 2005) allows teachers to feature forms of motivation, implementation, environment, and negotiations (MIEN) to increase learner achievement, teacher self-efficacy, and curricular fulfillment within the educational enterprise. Pedagogical content can be thought of as the "how to teach" as well as the "why" of how to teach.

Assessment Content

In order for teachers to establish the purpose for and evidence of learning, teachers must align an assessment with the content and pedagogy. Teachers may think of assessment content as "why to teach and learn." The teacher, learner, and learner's parents must understand what is being learned (academic content or curriculum), how it will be learned (pedagogical content or instruction), why it is being learned and ways the learning will be expressed (assessment content), and the connections to college, career, community, and civic life (learner content).

The growing attention on learners' engagement and achievement must be accompanied by growing attention on the teacher's analysis and efficacy. Candidates and teachers can no longer presume that assessment is merely another aspect of pedagogy and that the outcomes are limited to learner productivity.

Assessment content encompasses four overarching purposes: the measurement of (1) the teacher's thoroughness, (2) the learners' achievements, (3) the schooling policies and practices, and (4) the framing (Connell, 2010) of the entire educational context. All four perspectives are required to obtain and analyze the complete picture for enhancing teacher self-efficacy.

Data analyses should reveal the strengths and weaknesses applicable to teaching, learning, schooling, and framing related to motivation, implementation, environment, and negotiations (MEIN). Assessment content can be thought of as the "when of how to teach."

Learner Content

Academic, pedagogical, and assessment contents are static without their being contextualized within the dynamics of the learners. Candidates and teachers must be cognizant of the learner content that they establish and nurture. It is imperative that candidates and teachers know their learners as individuals and as members of peer groups, family structures, and religious organizations with cultural characteristics and learning strengths and talents.

Learners convey a particular set of norms and expectations almost universal in nature. Learners fully understand the environment and quickly adopt both the communicated and hidden curriculum of the school through observation and/or orientation.

Each teacher brings an individual teaching style that includes the teacher's level of intelligence; register of language; abilities to integrate the content naturally, especially through various forms of literacy; connections with the world that the learners may or may not have experienced; pedagogical expertise giving learners time to think; opportunities to talk with peers; and experiences to express learning via multiple learning styles, co-construct new knowledge, personalize new ideas, and so forth.

Some teachers frame the classroom as a shared community of learners both encouraging and welcoming learners' contributions, while other teachers refer to the classroom as belonging to the teacher and maintaining strict adherence to a predetermined schedule and delivery style. The teacher's MIEN plays a significant role in the classroom content.

Learners' interests are imperative to plan and facilitate the context of the academic, pedagogical, and assessment content. They convey a sense of place where everyone feels safe, welcome, and excited about learning, growing, sharing, and caring. The classroom content should link the classroom with the world—locally and globally. Teachers may think of learner and classroom content as "where to teach and learn."

MADISON'S PROFICIENCY WITH ACADEMIC, PEDAGOGICAL, ASSESSMENT, AND LEARNER CONTENT

Madison's early appraisal of her knowledge and skills and her understanding that teacher effectiveness is the primary influence on learner achievement revealed the necessity for her to fortify her academic, pedagogical, assessment, and learner content to enhance her self-efficacy. These insights highlight two essential teacher characteristics (Kukla-Acevedo, 2009; Schön, 1995) that matter: self-assessment and self-efficacy.

Although most success and satisfaction is associated with teacher education and experience (both during preparation and continuing during the profession), discursive awareness and critical consciousness generating self-assessment and self-efficacy of content are the two most important elements that need to emerge for candidates and teachers to demonstrate proficiency. Once Madison appraised her academic, pedagogical, assessment, and learner content honestly and holistically and took steps to enhance her self-efficacy naturally and authentically, she was ready to become the best teacher possible.

DISCUSSION QUESTIONS

1. What concerns do teacher candidates possess about becoming a teacher?
2. What concerns do you think career teachers possess about enhancing their effectiveness?

3. What does self-efficacy mean to you?
4. How are effectiveness and self-efficacy alike? How are they different?
5. How well are you prepared for academic, pedagogical, assessment, and learner content? What do you need to be better prepared?

ADDITIONAL RESOURCES

An Introduction to Self-Efficacy. http://www.gifted.uconn.edu/siegle/selfefficacy/section1.html.

Teacher Self-Efficacy Scale. http://u.osu.edu/hoy.17/files/2014/09/Bandura-Instr-1sdm5sg.pdf.

Survey Instruments to Help You in Your Investigations of Schools. http://mxtsch.people.wm.edu/research_tools.php.

REFERENCES

Aaronson, D., Barrow, L., & Sander, W. (2007). Teachers and student achievement in the Chicago public high schools. *Journal of Labor Economics, 25*(1), 95–135.

American Federation of Teachers. (2010). *American academic: A national survey of part time/adjunct faculty* (Vol. 2). Washington, DC: American Federation of Teachers. Retrieved from http://webcache.googleusercontent.com/search?q=cache:Uusx4OunFjUJ:www.aft.org/sites/default/files/aa_partimefaculty0310.pdf+&cd=1&hl=en&ct=clnk&gl=us.

Arum, R., & Roska, J. (2010). *Academically adrift: Limited learning on college campuses.* Chicago, IL: University of Chicago Press.

Auguste, B., Kihn, P., & Miller, M. (2010). *Closing the talent gap: Attracting and retaining top-third graduates to careers in teaching.* Washington, DC: McKinsey & Company.

Bandura, A., (1977). Self-efficacy: Toward a unifying theory of behavioral change. *Psychological Review, 84*(2), 191–215.

Black, P., Harrison, C., Lee, C., Marshall, B., & Wiliam, D. (2004). Working inside the black box: Assessment for learning in the classroom. *Phi Delta Kappan, 86*(1), 9–21.

Clotfelter, C. T., Ladd, H. F., & Vigdor, J. L. (2010). Teacher credentials and student achievement in high school: A cross-subject analysis with student fixed effects. *The Journal of Human Resources. 45*(3), 665–81.

Connell, M. T. (2010). Framing teacher education: Participation frameworks as resources for teacher learning, *Pedagogies: An International Journal, 5*(2), 87–106.

Czerniak, C. M. (1990). *A study of self-efficacy, anxiety, and science knowledge in preservice elementary teachers.* Paper presented at the National Association for Research in Science Teaching, Atlanta, GA.

Davies, R., & Osguthorpe, R. T. (2003) Reflecting on Learner Intent. *Reflective Practice, 4*(3) 131–40.

Erikson, E. H. (1950). *Childhood and society.* New York, NY: Norton.

Feistritzer, C. E. (2010). *Profile of teachers in the US.* Washington, DC: National Center for Education Information. Retrieved from http://www.edweek.org/media/pot2011final-blog.pdf.

Gallavan, N. P. (2007). Seven perceptions that influence novice teachers' efficacy and cultural competence. *Journal of Praxis in Multicultural Education, 2*(1), 6–22.

Gallavan, N. P. (2011). *Examining our own practices with purpose and passion: Commission on teacher self-efficacy.* Paper presented at the annual meeting of the Association of Teacher Educators, Orlando, FL.

Gallavan, N. P., & Webster-Smith, A. (2012). Cultural competence and the recursive nature of conscientization. In N. P. Gallavan and C. E. Craig (Eds.), *Issues in education; Part I.* ATE Yearbook XXI (pp. 401–19). Philadelphia, PA: Taylor & Francis.

Koedel, C. (2011). *Grade inflation for education majors and low standards for teachers. American Enterprise Institute.* Retrieved from http://www.aei.org/article/education/k-12/grade-inflation-for-education-majors-and-low-standards-for-teachers/.

Kukla-Acevedo, S. (2009). Do teacher characteristics matter? New results on the effects of teacher preparation on student achievement. *Economics of Education Review, 28*, 49–57.

Levine, A. (2006). *Educating school teachers.* Washington, DC: The Education Schools Project. Retrieved from http://www.edschools.org/teacher_report.htm.

National Commission on Teaching and America's Future (NCTAF). (2010) *Who will teach? Experience matters.* Retrieved from http://nctaf.org/wp-content/uploads/2012/01/NCTAF-Who-Will-Teach-Experience-Matters-2010-Report.pdf.

Rinaldo, V. J., Denig, S. J., Sheeran, T. J., Cramer-Benjamin, R., Vermette, P. J., Foote, C. J., & Smith, R. M. (2009). Developing the intangible qualities of good teaching: A self-study. *Education, 130*(1), 42–52.

Ross, J. A., & Bruce, C. D. (2007). Teacher self-assessment: A mechanism for facilitating professional growth. *Teaching & Teacher Education, 23*(2), 146–59.

Schön, D. A. (1983). *The reflective practitioner: How professionals think in action.* New York, NY: Basic Books.

Schön, D. A. (1995). Knowing in action. The new scholarship requires a new epistemology. *Change, 27*(6) 27–34.

Shulman, L. (1986). Those who understand: Knowledge growth in teaching. *Educational Researcher, 15*(2), 4–14.

Shulman, L. (1987). Knowledge and teaching: Foundations of the new reform. *Harvard Educational Review, 57*(1), 1–22.

Shulman, L. (1992). Ways of seeing, ways of knowing, ways of teaching, ways of learning about teaching. *Journal of Curriculum Studies, 28*, 393–96.

Swackhamer, L. E., Koellner, K., Basile, C., & Kimbrough, D. (2009). Increasing the self-efficacy of inservice teachers through content knowledge. *Teacher Education Quarterly, 36*(2), 63–78.

United States Census Bureau. (2012). *Field of bachelor degrees in the United States: 2009.* Retrieved from http://www.census.gov/prod/2012pubs/acs-18.pdf.

The Wallace Foundation. (2008). *Becoming a leader: Preparing school principals for today's schools.* New York, NY: The Wallace Foundation.

Wiggins, G. P., & McTighe, J. (2005). *Understanding by design* (expanded 2nd ed.). Alexandria, VA: Association of Curriculum and Supervision Development.

Chapter Five

The Interactive Dual Impact of Teacher Self-Efficacy and Creative Self-Efficacy on 21st-Century Student Creative and Innovative Performance and Potentiality

Elizabeth Johnson and Mary Kathleen Walsh

The bell rings and students shuffle into the classroom, some reluctantly and some with the great enthusiasm that a new school year brings. As the students take their seats, they notice a word written boldly across the whiteboard, "RELENTLESS." The teacher, new to the building but not to the profession, decided that she needed to start the year with a clear message to the students about her expectations with a focus on powerful student learning.

This urban, Title 1 school is known for consistent failing grades, low-performing students, and their teachers who struggle to achieve a high rating on their teacher evaluation document. When Mrs. N was hired, she was adamant that this failure was not going to continue. Her desire was to indelibly mark the students' minds with a message of hope and an unrelenting attitude that there is no room for giving up! This was a belief she manifested every day with every student.

It took three months for her students to realize that she meant what she said. She created a learning environment where the students knew she believed in them every step of the way. With this, they gained more voice, confidence, and vision for their potential. She was very strategic in her efforts to allow every student to feel successful and be completely accountable for their own learning process. She never wavered. Many nights she would drive home in tears because of how exhaustively challenging the day was.

The students saw their teacher as RELENTLESS! As a result of this determination, love, and fortitude, they would walk into her classroom every day stating that they were ready to learn. They encouraged each other to strive toward the mark, and they supported the learning environment that Mrs. N had strategically created for them. By the end of the year, their grades had moved from an E to A's, B's, and C's. Her strategies and beliefs had improved the scores in her classroom over 300 percent! How did Mrs. N achieve such remarkable success? A closer look into her classroom reveals her strategies and power of her pedagogy.

Daniel Pink (2008), author of the *New York Times* best-selling book *A Whole New Mind: Why Right Brain Thinkers Will Rule the Future*, advocates that the great shift of the early twenty-first century is from left to right. Rather than being a political change, however, Pink's shift is uniquely centered on the brain, where gifted right-brained learners, that is, the "artists, inventors, storytellers, caregivers, consolers and big picture people," will rule (p. 1).

Pink argues that this century represents the zealous triumph of our creative and innovative right brain over the more procedural and linear thinking of our left brain (ibid.). His provocative book implies that the most critical element to catapult performance and satisfaction within any context is within our deep inner drive to direct our own destiny coupled with the ability to envision and create new entities that better serve humankind.

His research supports the premises set forth in Thomas Friedman's groundbreaking book, *The World Is Flat*, by exploring what he classifies as having the "right stuff" (2005, p. 308). He delineates that "the right stuff is inclusive of the educational competencies needed to survive in a flattened world and more importantly, the availability of the current education paradigm to build robust right-brain skills over those that can be easily duplicated by technology and linear paradigms" (ibid.). He further states that there is an "excitingly new 21st century skillset that must be attained within today's globalized and highly interconnected flattened world" (ibid).

INTRODUCTION

This chapter investigates the profound impact of teachers' self-efficacy on their own creative and innovative work and how that may be a strong predictor of student academic and creative performance and potentiality. Furthermore, this chapter explores the connection between higher teacher self-efficacy and creative self-efficacy coupled with how humans are driven by a hunger for innovative and creative work.

The authors strive to unfold and articulate a response to this chapter's essential question: Do teachers with higher self-efficacy exhibit and engender greater levels of creative and innovative pedagogical behaviors, and how does this correlate to increased student academic and creative performance and productivity? In addition, this chapter provides a response to the query: What does this really mean for teacher educators as we meet the exhaustive demands of preparing our twenty-first-century diverse cadre of learners to wonderfully thrive within our very challenging global society and flattened world?

THE SETTING

We will begin this chapter by getting acquainted with a seasoned teacher who is embarking on her first year of teaching in a school setting that many see as having insurmountable odds for academic growth and achievement.

Mrs. N creates a robust twenty-first-century, creative learning environment. But where is Mrs. N? She is not in the classroom. She is standing by the entrance door greeting her students and giving each of them the secret class handshake. What is going on? She doesn't look like a normal teacher; rather, she is dressed completely in full-body Northern Outfitters–brand extreme-weather outdoor clothing including a beautiful furry hood and thick woven gloves. And what is this next to her but an Alaskan husky, a very large dog with well-groomed and pristine white and black fur, standing very majestically by her side.

The children come in and are overwhelmed with joy, excitement, and wonderment and cannot take their eyes off Mrs. N and her sidekick! Something is surely going to rock and roll this learning environment! As she shuts the door, she addresses her students:

Good morning "Mighty Mushers"! The famous Iditarod Dog Sledding Race Trail covering 1,150 miles begins every March in Anchorage, Alaska. We are all going to be a part of this renowned race! As you can see, I am dressed ready for the frigid outdoors. My outfit allows me to be outside in the elements where I can survive in 80 degrees below zero weather. I am ready to lead my sled dogs through this dangerous adventure called, "The Last Greatest Race on Earth." Meet my lead sled dog, Brutus, who has been with me for 15 years. He is a huge Alaskan Husky who trains with me. Without the lead sled dog, many mushers would not survive!

Over the next several months as we work in our teams, we will be preparing for this race. We will be accomplishing this death-defying feat by working in our "Professional Learning Teams (PLT)" and utilizing both our virtual classroom and outdoor learning centers as well as experiencing diverse community terrains to train and execute many skills around dog sled-

ding and winter survival. Daily we will be online and experiencing the "Idit-arod Race News Center" updates and watching live videos of the mushers and their amazing dogs.

We, too, will upload our own "live" videos from our learning centers to their official race website and conduct daily data analyses including weather conditions, terrain hazards, sled dog nutritional and health needs for dogs and mushers, geographical challenges, and updates from the various race checkpoints to name only a few of our tasks that are ahead of us.

Your PLC teams will be using the state math, literacy, social studies, science, technology and physical education standards and skillsets to accomplish these tasks and to research and report on the Iditarod. One example of what your PLC Team will be doing is investigating the physical and psychological impact of the extreme Alaskan weather and terrains on the participants. Throughout, your team will be creating and recalibrating powerful essential questions that will drive a culminating newscast inclusive of data portrayed in visual, auditory, and written form along with your findings using "on-the-scene" reporting and interviews.

So, mount your sleds and hold tight to your reins and let's give the command now to our sled dog teams as we can start our PLC Team races. Ready? Repeat after me the very words that all Iditarod mushers say before they begin: Mush! Hike! All Right? Let's Go!

LITERATURE REVIEW AND DRIVING QUESTIONS

Before deconstructing and drawing inferences from the narrative of Mrs. N with regard to the essential question stated earlier in this chapter, it is important to select the lenses and key concepts and questions upon which to examine the power of her pedagogical artistry. A review of the literature as it relates to the concepts of creativity, innovation, and teacher and creative self-efficacy aligns with the work of both Daniel Pink and Thomas Friedman.

The National Center on Education and the Economy (NCEE) published their *Research Summary and Final Report* titled "The Sources of Innovation and Creativity," which reflected what Adams (2005) called "a comprehensive summary of current research and theory on the sources of innovation and creativity, both in individuals and organizations" (p. 1).

Researchers have put forth recommendations on how educational systems can foster the attributes of innovation and creativity within students. The following queries are extracted from that report. These key questions are ones that must be addressed first and should be the driving force for our educational decisions within the framework of a global economy. According to Adams, the following are reflective of key questions to drive a discussion on the sources of innovation and creativity:

1. What do we know about the sources of creativity and innovation in individuals?
2. What do we know about the curricula and pedagogical techniques that have been proven effective in promoting innovation and creativity through formal and informal education?
3. What do we know about techniques that have been proven to stimulate creativity and innovation in the workplace?
4. What is it about the nature of our culture, our society and our economy that makes our country more creative and innovative than others?
5. What contributes to the development of successful entrepreneurs?
6. What actions should the US education system take to promote innovation and creativity among students?
7. What are some suggestions for further research? (2005, p. 2)

The questions posed by Adams are paramount for every educator and district in prioritizing decisions about preparing twenty-first-century learners in competing within our global world. Within the Adams article, questions one through three are addressed in Mrs. N's pedagogical context. Her creativity and innovation intersect with her pedagogy and are juxtaposed with her philosophy and her continued drive to showcase this within her workplace. Questions four and five call into attention the nature of school culture and its effects on engendering creativity and innovation coupled with the development of entrepreneurs.

The school that Mrs. N is teaching in has a current culture of school failure coupled with families living in poverty; a social reproduction, which evidences little support for creativity, innovation, and entrepreneurship. Questions six and seven support the critical need for continued research in the conceptualization and operationalization of mandating and funding institutions of learning, driven by principles that prioritize successful entrepreneurs within the twenty-first century.

Dr. Teresa Amabile (1998), head of the Entrepreneurial Management Unit at Harvard Business School, advocates that creativity ascends through the convergence of three elements:

1. *Knowledge*: All the relevant understanding an individual brings to bear on a creative effort.
2. *Creative Thinking*: Relates to how people approach problems and depends on personality and thinking/working style.
3. *Motivation*: Motivation is generally accepted as key to creative production, with the most important motivators being intrinsic passion and interest in the work itself (p. 2).

Amabile continues, "Within every individual, creativity is a function of three components: expertise, creative-thinking skills, and motivation. Can managers influence these components? The answer is an emphatic yes—for better or for worse—through workplace practices and conditions" (p. 2).

When applying Amabile's "Three Components of Creativity," one can vividly see that Mrs. N artfully and purposefully operationalizes these innovations through what is called "professional learning teams." These teams view themselves as professional learners whose role is to solve problems by using real-life events and virtual resources to widen their knowledge. Mrs. N approaches problems in a contextualized manner and uses a number of techniques to invite and ignite. Mrs. N is well aware of the school culture, and her disposition shows an "abundant evidence of strong intrinsic motivation " (Amabile, 1998, p. 6).

Finally, Amabile reminds us, "Expertise and creative thinking are an individual's raw material—his or her natural resources, if you will" (ibid., p. 3). Perhaps the most defining element that drives and facilitates Mrs. N's pedagogy is that of her "raw" inner core natural resources coupled with a "work style that uses 'incubation'" (ibid.).

Another lens used to observe Mrs. N's narrative is that of self-efficacy. According to Bandura (2007), one's perception of self-efficacy is

> best conceptualized as *perceived operative capability.* It focuses on the belief in what *someone can do* with whatever resources one can muster—rather than with what *someone has.* The operative nature of perceived self-efficacy is an integral feature of the procedure used to access people's efficacy beliefs. Individuals are not asked to rate the *abilities they possess,* but rather the strength of their assurance they *can execute* given activities under designated situational demands. (p. 646)

Adding to Bandura's conception, Axtell and Parker (2003) state that "self-efficacy refers to people's judgments about their capability to perform particular tasks. Task-related self-efficacy increases the effort and persistence towards challenging tasks; therefore, increasing the likelihood that they will be completed" (p. 114).

Tierney and Farmer (2002) point out that "Bandura (1997) cited strong self-efficacy as a necessary condition for creative productivity and the discovery of new knowledge. The concept of self-efficacy holds much promise for understanding creative action in organizational settings" (p. 1137). Interestingly enough, this article "addresses the joint impact of dual efficacy [self and creative] in relation to creativity providing a more complex view of the self-efficacy-performance association" (ibid.).

Mrs. N's usage and modeling of self-efficacy and creative self-efficacy (CSE) is chronicled in the narrative. It is further evident that Mrs. N is in complete alignment with the work of both Pink and Friedman, all within the context of embracing and aligning what Pink calls "right-brain" skills that juxtapose with what Friedman terms "the right stuff." Each of these components is within the context of preparing students for meeting the challenges of both our global society and flattened world.

Mrs. N's creative self-efficacy is evidenced within the Model Core Teaching Standards (CCSSO, 2011), which "outlines what all teachers across all content and grade levels should know and be able to do to be effectively in today's learning contexts. They are a revision of the 1992 model standards, in response to the needs of the next generation learners" (ibid., p. 1). This chapter and the content within it align to the following InTASC Standards for pedagogical performance and have great implications for innovation and creativity within twenty-first-century learning:

- Standard #6: Assessment. The teacher understands and uses multiple methods of assessment to engage learners in their own growth, to monitor learner progress, and to guide the teacher's and learner's decision-making.
- Standard #7: Planning for Instruction. The teacher plans instruction that supports every student in meeting rigorous learning goals by drawing upon knowledge of content areas, curriculum, cross-disciplinary skills, and pedagogy, as well as knowledge of learners and the community context.
- Standard #8: Instructional Strategies. The teacher understands and uses a variety of instructional strategies to encourage learners to develop deep understanding of content areas and their connections, and to build skills to apply knowledge in meaningful ways. (ibid., pp. 15–17).

These standards have many powerful implications for teacher educators. When creative self-efficacy and self-efficacy are added into the equation, it's a "win-win" situation for all involved—students, teachers, and schools—a mighty triangulation!

CONCLUSION

The authors have examined the essential questions at the beginning of their article, "Do Teachers with Higher Self-Efficacy Exhibit and Engender Greater Levels of Creative and Innovative Pedagogical Behaviors, and How Does This Correlate to Increased Student Academic and Creative Performance and Productivity?" and concluded that teachers who possess a high level of self-efficacy and creative self-efficacy are more enabled and empowered to engender a vibrant learning experience in which students and teachers showcase creative innovations that increase student growth and achievement while aligning with InTASC Standards #6–8.

REFLECTION QUESTIONS

1. What do you believe about the integrity and merit of every student in your classroom?
2. How does your pedagogy align with your students' abilities to create a twenty-first-century innovative and creative work product?
3. Considering Pink's and Friedman's beliefs that this century is truly a right-brained century, what creative and innovative strategies are you using that build on the efficacy of the students?
4. How do you, as a teacher, exhibit and engender high levels of creativity and innovation in your own pedagogy, and how do your assessments showcase this creativity?
5. How often do you allow your students to be self-directed as you change your role from bringing forth knowledge and information to facilitator of student discovery of knowledge?
6. What kind of creative and innovative expressions do you allow your students to have in math and science?
7. Strong efficacy beliefs alone cannot increase creative performance, but weak efficacy beliefs can and will have a negative impact on creative performance. Therefore, how do you see yourself helping your students recalibrate their creative self-efficacy?
8. How do you see yourself reflected in the vignette that was given early on in this chapter? Give some examples of how you inspire your students to be innovative and creative thinkers.

EDUCATOR RESOURCES AND RESOURCE DISCUSSION QUESTIONS

1. www.criticalthinking.org

This is the world's longest running annual conference on critical thinking. This website offers a myriad of tools that can assist teachers and students in fostering critical thinking in both teaching and learning. It can assist the teacher in facilitating self-directed learning as well as bring forth many creative strategies to be used in the classroom.

What strategies did Mrs. N use to create an environment driven by critical thinking?

2. http://www.p21.org

Every child in the United States needs twenty-first-century skills in order to be productive citizens and leaders. This coalition brings together the business community and education leaders and policy makers to center U.S. K–12 education with the skills needed for this competitive global world. It includes

the five essential ingredients needed for school success: student voice, an engaged community, distributed leadership, a climate of achievement, and evidence and research.
What twenty-first-century skills did you see evidence of within the pedagogy of Mrs. N?

3. http://www.un.org/millenniumgoals/
The United Nations Millennium Development Goals address a set of common world challenges agreed upon by the world's countries and leading development institutions and target them for eradication by combining the efforts of all governments, societies, and organizations. Using these goals in the classroom helps to prepare a student's mind for a global thought process, problem solving, and creative thinking.
How can teachers infuse the eight Millennium Development Goals within a creative framework and engender powerful and meaningful student creative and academic performance?

4. http://www.ted.com/talks/simon_sinek_how_great_leaders_inspire_action
Simon Sinek's TED talk discusses the powerful model for inspirational leadership. His ideas regarding innovation and creativity explore the *whys*, *hows*, and *whats* of our decisions. What if we were to teach like this? Explore this using Simon Sinek's model to drive innovation, creative teaching, and learning.
How does the "Golden Circle" become a mechanism to drive my learning environment?

5. https://www.youtube.com/watch?v=H0_yKBitO8M
Tom Wujec and The Marshmallow Challenge
Consider this activity that not only builds teamwork and collaboration in your classroom, it also explores the idea of prototypes and the nature of collaboration, concepts needed for creative thinking and exploring. Correlate this to your classroom practices and discover how powerful it is to facilitate an activity that allows your students to drive their own learning while helping students identify hidden assumptions.
How can I utilize this exercise in building prototypes driven by innovation and creativity?

REFERENCES

Adams, K. (2005). *The sources of innovation and creativity.* The National Center on Education and the Economy, ERIC No. ED522111.
Amabile, T. M. (1998). September-October). How to kill creativity. *Harvard Business Review,* 76-87.

Axtell, C., and Parker, S. (2003). Promoting role breadth self-efficacy through involvement, work redesign and training. *Human Relations, 56*(1), 113–31.

Bandura, A. (2007). Much ado over faulty conception of perceived self-efficacy grounded in faulty experimentation. *Journal of Social and Clinical Psychology, 26*(6), 641–758.

Council of Chief State School Officers. (2011). *A resource for state dialogue.* Retrieved from http://www.ccsso.org/Documents/2011/InTASC_Model_Core_Teaching_Standards_2011.pdf.

Friedman, T. (2005). *The world is flat: A brief history of the twenty-first century.* New York, NY: Farrar, Straus and Giroux.

Pink, D. (2008). *A whole new mind: Why right brain thinkers will rule the future.* New York, NY: The Berkley Publishing Group.

Tierney, P., & Farmer, S. M. (2002). Creative self-efficacy: Potential antecedents and relationship to creative performance. *Academy of Management Journal, 45*, 1137–48.

Chapter Six

Challenge

Efficacious Teachers View Obstacles as Opportunities

Walter Polka, Amanda Fernandes, Elissa Smith, and Kylie Flynn

Difficulty strengthens the mind, as labor does the body.—Lucius Annaeus Seneca

"I don't understand why he's acting this way. I've tried everything to get him to sit and pay attention during instruction," she added, exasperated. "Tell me about what you've tried so far," prompted Marco, a veteran teacher of nearly a decade. "I moved Aiden to sit by a positive peer, I've contacted mom about his behavior, I've used our progressive discipline tool—there's nothing left to do!" Sophia replied, frustrated. "Tell me more about Aiden," encouraged Marco. "You've told me a lot about what Aiden does, but can you tell me more about who he is?" asked Marco. "I'm not sure what you're asking," confessed Sophia nervously.

Initial Reflective Thoughts: Upon reading the start of the case presented above, reflect on Sophia's experience. *Challenge* can be presented in many ways and at varying degrees. Categorize the case into the different types of *Challenge* this teacher faced. How would you divide the various sources of *Challenge* being presented? Which type of *Challenge* is the most exigent? How might you react to these forms of *Challenge*?

Smiling, Marco shared, "I find it really helpful to first think about who my students are before I try to plan for what they can do. What do they enjoy? What barriers are they faced with daily? What environment do they encounter when they leave school? All those pieces play into why they act the way they do and help me to figure out what motivates them as learners." Tilting her head a bit, Sophia inquisitively pushed Marco for more details,

57

asking how to figure out those tidbits of information, and how personal information should impact planning and instruction. She remained open to the information shared by her colleague and mentor, Marco.

Marco summarized how he has been so successful in engaging students who traditionally struggle. "Building relationships with students and learning what drives them is important when dealing with all students, but it is critical when dealing with challenging students and situations. When the environment in the classroom is one of mutual respect and rapport, when lessons have been individualized for students' needs and interests, it becomes easier for them to become engaged in the material. Also, always remember students at all levels of the educational spectrum don't care how much the teacher knows until they know how much the teacher cares!"

Before she returned to her own classroom, Marco encouraged Sophia to be self-reflective as she planned for the following week. She decided to start by greeting all her students on Monday with a warm welcome to be sure to start the week off well, and she added a few "getting to know you" questions to the traditional activity she had previously planned. As she packed her bag on Sunday evening, she also added a brief thank-you note for Marco, encouraging him to ask her about the activity so they could debrief the lesson later that week.

Additional Reflection: Reflect on Sophia's resolution to the *Challenge* placed before her. How would you evaluate Sophia's self-efficacy as a teacher based on her reactions? How do your proposed reactions compare to Sophia's? Since self-efficacy concerns one's sense of accomplishment, how might Sophia feel about the outcome of the presented situation? How might varying degrees of self-efficacy result in different outcomes?

> The greater the obstacle, the more glory in overcoming it.—Molière

Being able to successfully nurture the disposition of *Challenge* is in direct relationship to a developed sense of self-efficacy. To varying degrees, educators are constantly faced with challenges. Developing self-efficacy as an educator involves being able to continuously improve upon one's ability to interact with and overcome *Challenge*.

SELF-EFFICACY AND THE EFFECTIVE TEACHER

Self-efficacy is an individual's belief in personal capabilities to produce designated levels of performance, influencing events that affect the individual's life and determining the individual's feelings, thoughts, words, actions, and interactions. Strong self-efficacy enhances one's sense of accomplishment and well-being (Bandura, 1997). Additionally, Ormond (2006) has identified self-efficacy as the extent or strength of one's own ability to complete tasks and reach goals.

Teacher self-efficacy shapes a "teacher's judgments about her or his abilities to promote student learning" (Hoy & Spero, 2005, p. 1) by enhancing one's awareness and actions for taking responsibility for student engagement and outcomes (Dembo & Gibson, 1985). Therefore, it is essential for teacher educators to develop and foster the knowledge, skills, and dispositions associated with teacher self-efficacy throughout their teacher-education-program courses and field experiences. Furthermore, all practicing teachers need to reinforce their acute sense of *Challenge* throughout their career to further enhance their self-efficacy.

SELF-EFFICACY AND *CHALLENGE*

Consistent with the accepted definition of self-efficacy, the idea of *Challenge* plays a significant role in the success of a teacher. A sense of *Challenge* in this profession communicates the confidence of teachers in their ability to observe difficulties as opportunities that may be used to accomplish current tasks and future goals. Teachers with a strong sense of *Challenge* regularly make use of obstacles to build on existing strengths toward positive achievements rather than perceiving them as crises (Csikszentmihalyi, 1990). The importance of high self-efficacy in teachers to produce positive student outcomes was also emphasized by Bandura (1997).

Today's diverse student populations require motivated teachers willing to face the challenge of planning for instruction that meets the needs of these diverse learners. Consistent with InTASC Standard #7, which amplifies the importance of this challenge, "The teacher plans instruction that supports every student in meeting rigorous learning goals by drawing upon knowledge of content areas, curriculum, cross-disciplinary skills, and pedagogy, as well as knowledge of learners and the community context" (CCSSO, 2011, p. 16).

EXPERIENCING EDUCATIONAL CHALLENGES

> If you aren't in over your head, how do you know how tall you are?—T. S. Eliot

Experiencing *Challenge* occurs when a teacher is faced with a difficult or new situation, or changes in the expected environment. *Challenge* can be presented in many ways and in varying degrees. The context in which *Challenge* is presented will also affect the outcomes of the situation. Regardless of the severity, intensity, or reoccurrence of the *Challenge*, a self-efficacious teacher will use the same set of personal approaches to overcome it.

Self-efficacy relates to one's ability to exercise control over life circumstances (Bandura, 1977). The social cognitive theory based on agency suggests that to be an agent is to "exert intentional influence on one's functioning and the course of events by one's actions" (Bandura, 2012, p. 11). Thus, self-efficacy encompasses this framework. Additionally, developing self-efficacy through improving one's reactions to *Challenge* will "predict both teacher practices and student learning" (Skaalvik & Skaalvik, 2007, p. 611). The benefits of increasing one's self-efficacy become increasingly important as teachers are exposed to new challenging situations.

Persons act in certain ways because they think their actions will result in certain outcomes and because they believe in their own abilities to perform such actions (Evans, 2012). As a result, being able to foster a positive sense of *Challenge* will allow teachers to increase their self-efficacy in knowing how to react and in being able to respond to the various challenges presented in their personal and professional lives.

Persons with a highly developed disposition of *Challenge* accept challenges and adversity as an integral part of their experiences (Polka, 2010b). Teachers with a strong sense of *Challenge* have the belief that they can continue to learn from challenges and that facing such challenges will further develop a personal set of approaches to successfully overcome future challenges in their personal and professional lives. Keeping in mind that teachers are also leaders, Cashman (2008) supports the notion that successful leaders know there is no end-point to growing authentically.

Challenge should not be considered as merely surviving the tough situations, the disputes, the questions, or the conflicts teachers face. The concept of *Challenge* supersedes these everyday encounters. A strong sense of *Challenge* is the ability to face a crisis and turn it into an opportunity (Polka, 2010b). Though *Challenge* is presented in various ways, teachers are most commonly faced with four particular forms of *Challenge*.

Types of Educational Challenge

The environment teachers are exposed to is not static; it is extremely variable and in a constant state of flux. Though the many forms of *Challenge* teachers face are diverse, there are four classifications that are consistently cited as being significant sources of *Challenge* (Holzberger, Philipp, & Kunter, 2013; Kelm & McIntosh, 2012; Masunaga & Lewis, 2011; Olli-Pekke et al., 2013; Skaalvik and Skaalvik, 2007). Accordingly, the following four categories are the educational *Challenges* most commonly faced by teachers:

1. Instructional Programming *w/ differentiation*
2. Classroom Management
3. Student Engagement

4. Peer and Parental Cooperation

Instructional programming. Instructional programming is a reality for all teachers. Whether one has to follow a guide or create new learning experiences, the necessity to meet students' needs is imperative. *Challenge* is often met while planning for instructional programming (Olli-Pekke et al., 2013). Being an effective teacher often revolves around the ability to create educational experiences that are flexible enough to adapt to the needs of differentiated learners (Holzberger, Philipp, & Kunter, 2013; Kelm & McIntosh, 2012).

Nevertheless, effective teachers will often still strive to meet all students' needs (Johnson et al., 1991). Attempting to meet such a variety of needs can present *Challenges* to teachers (Kelm & McIntosh, 2012). Furthermore, having to conform to a predetermined curriculum that requires teachers to organize "teaching in ways one did not believe [are] the best" (Skaalvik & Skaalvik, 2007, p. 621) creates *Challenge* in need of being overcome.

Classroom management. Aside from constricting instructional programming while attempting to meet diverse student skills and needs, problem behavior, which negatively impacts classroom management, is cited as another source of *Challenge* for teachers (Holzberger, Philipp & Kunter, 2013; Kelm & McIntosh, 2012; Skaalvik & Skaalvik, 2007). Though the level of disturbance may vary, from slight distractions to student assaults, discipline hindrances affect teachers' ability to perform.

Student engagement. *Challenge* can also be experienced when teachers note a lack of student interest and performance (Evans, 2012). A teacher with a strong sense of self-efficacy aims to meet students' needs (Johnson et al., 1991). Noting that students are not engaged or cooperative can be both frustrating and demoralizing. However, it also offers the teacher opportunities to reflect and improve their instruction for more effective student engagement.

Peer and parental cooperation. In addition to the various teacher-student interactions in the classroom, teachers must also regularly engage with other teachers and parents. Conflict stemming from opposing views or competition is also a source of *Challenge* (Skaalvik & Skaalvik, 2007; 2010). Additionally, diminished collaboration among teachers is associated with experiencing *Challenge* in the different stages of teaching service, for example, while student teaching or in performance-pay contracts, or working toward National Board Certification (Masunaga & Lewis, 2011).

Diminished *Challenge*

The stressors experienced by teachers are varied. As Betoret (2006) explains, "work overload, role ambiguity and conflict, pressures of the teacher's role, inadequate resources, poor working conditions, lack of professional recognition, low remuneration, lack of involvement in decision-making, lack of effective communication, staff conflicts, and pupil misbehavior" (p. 520) are all issues regularly faced by teachers. When teachers are asked about the types of *Challenge* they face, the above points are commonly cited.

The outcome of a diminished or weakened disposition of *Challenge* is burnout (Skaalvik & Skaalvik, 2007, 2010; Betoret, 2006). Burnout is characterized as experiencing persistent negative mental states, negative emotions and feelings, exhaustion, and the overall mindset of reduced competence (Betoret, 2006). Burnout is further defined as one's inability to continue coping with prolonged challenges (Jennet, Harris, & Mesibov, 2003). The consequences of burnout may be avoided by developing a positive and healthy sense of *Challenge* throughout one's career (Csikszentmihalyi, 1990; Litchka, Fenzel, & Polka, 2009; Patterson & Kelleher, 2005).

Developed *Challenge*

By recognizing *Challenge* in personal and professional lives, teachers are able to seek outcomes and activities that will result in a well-developed disposition of *Challenge*. In order to further nurture one's disposition of *Challenge*, one must first recognize and reflect upon one's current reactions to adversity and identify areas of both strength and weakness. Honest evaluations are required for this process to accomplish optimum effectiveness.

Transforming *Challenge* deficiencies into proficiencies can be accomplished through various activities including participating in mentoring relationships, debriefing events with colleagues, reviewing observations of practice, facilitating online interactions (blogs), and debriefing role-plays with colleagues (Rabey, 2014). A strong sense of *Challenge* is thus developed by increasing self-efficacy and reflection and by adopting a productive schoolwide atmosphere.

Increase self-efficacy. Increasing one's self-efficacy is likely to promote *Challenge*. In order to increase self-efficacy, teachers can increase their exposure to mastery and vicarious learning experiences (Evans, 2012; Olli-Pekke et al., 2013; Skaalvik & Skaalvik, 2007). Mastery and vicarious learning can be accomplished through training programs and observation of effective veteran teachers. Participating in mastery learning further helps promote resilience as teachers overcome obstacles (Bandura, 2012). Observing and discussing with others provides prior knowledge that can be incorporated into approaches to tackle future *Challenges*.

Reflection. Learning by observing or engaging in activities with others works best when reflection occurs. *Challenge* mastery is best developed in conjunction with others. Nevertheless, there is a need to be reflective about one's own experiences and reactions to *Challenge*. Engaging in self-reflection is accomplished when one self-evaluates on judgment choices in order to clarify meaning to better understand the context of the situation (Boyd & Fales, 1983).

Effective people are proactive (Covey, 1989). Such people learn from both positive and negative past experiences (Cashman, 2008). By engaging in reflection, teachers develop the disposition of *Challenge* by taking responsibility for their choices and their subsequent consequences. Also, increasing one's exposure to diverse and unique experiences while being cautious and reflective allows teachers to face future *Challenge* by referring to previous successes and building upon them.

School-wide atmosphere. Adopting a school-wide positive support system concerns promoting a positive school environment that "can facilitate success in teaching and learning, increased desired behaviors in students, and decreased instances of problem behaviors" (Kelm & McIntosh, 2012, p. 139). Incorporating resources of the school as a whole and creating a support system that allows "access to school coping resources (school equipment, didactic supplies, and qualified personnel for student support such as psychologists, speech therapists, resource specialist teachers, etc.)" protects teachers against stressors (Betoret, 2006, p. 534).

COMMENTS FROM THE FIELD

To further illustrate the importance of *Challenge* development for the promotion of teacher self-efficacy, the following teacher comments are included. These comments are representative of the personal educational experiences of teacher educators as identified in a qualitative study conducted at three North American universities (Niagara University, Missouri State University, and the University of Arkansas). These comments about the relationship between *Challenge* and self-efficacy exemplify how important a well-developed disposition of *Challenge* is to the field of education.

The qualitative study from which these responses were collected was aimed at examining current teacher-educator perspectives about student-teacher/teacher candidate self-efficacy (Polka, Pearman, & Bowles, 2011). The study's participants ($N = 62$) consisted of teacher educators belonging to multiple categories: professors ($N = 21$), associate professors ($N = 19$), assistant professors ($N = 6$), instructors ($N = 7$), part-time professors ($N = 5$), and supervisors ($N = 4$). Participants were experienced teacher educators in that most of them had over sixteen years of experience as teacher educators, with 29 percent of them having over twenty-five years of experience.

The following excerpts are representative responses to questions that asked participants to identify key characteristics and dispositions of teacher self-efficacy. These responses further demonstrate the need to develop a set of personal approaches for an enhanced sense of *Challenge*. Key connections related to the three ways of increasing one's sense of *Challenge* have been identified.

Increase Self-Efficacy

- *Teacher self-efficacy . . . manifests itself as teachers see the positive effects of their teaching and sense that their professional work counts for success. Such teachers are internally motivated to work at their own continuing professional development.*
- *Teacher takes responsibility for their own personal and professional development. Evidenced by the individual being a lifelong-learner and continuously contributing to the welfare of the school.*
- *Teacher self-efficacy is a teacher's perception of him/herself as being effective ... and having a significant degree of control over the quality of the teaching-learning process.*
- *Teacher self-efficacy develops over time, parallel to the development towards master teacher identity and respected professional status among peers.*

Reflection

- *Teacher self-efficacy is the ability to engage in reflective practice and consistently evaluate one's efficacy in relationship to identified goals.*
- *[Teacher self-efficacy] is the ability of the teacher to reflect on their instructional behaviors with students and make adjustments to improve. You see it in action when teachers monitor and adjust their instruction, sometimes immediately, to find those teachable moments that are meaningful to their students.*
- *Thoughtful and reflective regarding one's teaching preparation and the effectiveness of each lesson taught. Continuously seeking to improve as a teacher and fellow learner. Willing to try new things in the classroom.*
- *Teacher self-efficacy is like my reflection in the mirror. If I don't like what I see, I know it is up to me to make the necessary changes.*

School-Wide Atmosphere

- *Openness to constructive criticism for sake of growth.*
- *Empathetic, genuine, patient, resourceful, hopeful, hard-working, smart, team-player, life-long learner.*
- *Someone who is an active participant in the subject they are teaching, someone who motivates others.*

- *Willing to try new things in the classroom.*
- *A willingness . . . to learn about their community of learners needs to top the list.*
- *Personal connection to the community within the classroom as well as the school community.*
- *I believe that we will not be truly successful in educating students until we foster an accepting, comfortable, and welcoming atmosphere in all class-rooms.*

CONSTRUCTIVIST FOUNDATION

Teachers who are exemplars in *Challenge* development frequently use con-structivist perspectives to promote learners who link new knowledge with prior knowledge to further their understanding of new situations in an au-thentic manner (Foote, Vermette, & Battaglia, 2001). The notion of continu-ously evolving and using prior knowledge to seek creative solutions is direct-ly related to constructivist ideals (Polka, 2010a).

Constructivist principles include creating learning experiences that in-clude real-world situations that use social interactions to diversify learning, explore multiple representations of experiences, and implement cognitive and educational psychology principles (Sternberg and Williams, 2002). As mentioned earlier, engaging in mastery and diverse vicarious experiences in conjunction with reflective practices helps teachers build upon their disposi-tion toward *Challenge* by engaging in constructivist ideals.

CAREER-LONG BENEFITS OF CHALLENGE DEVELOPMENT

Life is either a daring adventure or nothing at all.—Helen Keller

The benefits of developing a career-long sense of *Challenge* go beyond the classroom. Teachers who develop their sense of *Challenge* look at life as a constant "challenge" and develop the ability to see change as an opportunity not a crisis. Persons with a strong sense of *Challenge* will help themselves and others make sense of situations as those challenging experiences evolve, as opposed to having prepackaged approaches to solving *Challenge* issues (Eggen & Kauchuk, 2001).

Subsequently, most teachers who have a well-developed *Challenge* dis-position will often apply constructivist approaches to their instructional pro-gramming, classroom management, and student engagement as well as to peer and parental interaction. The ability to recognize that one must progress with change will create a sense of confidence and self-efficacy as the disposi-tion of *Challenge* is developed or as Leon Megginson would aver when discussing Charles Darwin's work, "It is the not the strongest [species] that survives; but the species that survives is the one that is able to best adapt and adjust to the changing environment" (1963, p. 4).

Therefore, efficacious teachers view obstacles or challenges as opportunities to further evolve as a professional educator in terms of surviving and thriving in their ever-changing classroom environments. The first stop in this continuous professional evaluation is to develop a set of personal approaches as early as possible in one's career development, while recognizing that these approaches will change and emerge as new challenges present themselves. Enjoy the journey of becoming a self-efficacious teacher while recognizing that today's challenges only serve to advance one's professionalism.

DISCUSSION QUESTIONS

1. Describe a time when you were challenged to follow a prescribed curricular approach that you believed was not the best approach for your students. How did you react? How did you resolve the dilemma? Did you feel you had met the challenge in the interest of your students?
2. Discuss with your partner/group a challenging classroom management issue. How did the result affect your self-efficacy? What did you learn about yourself? Your students?
3. Describe a notable moment when you were able to inspire a student's interest or performance. Were you able to replicate the technique with other students or in other situations?
4. Discuss a scenario with your partner/group about a time when you perceived a lack of cooperation with peers or parents. What steps did you take to overcome the challenge? Did it convince the members to collaborate? What would you do differently if your efforts were ineffective?
5. Share how you maintain a strong sense of self-efficacy or how you plan to increase your self-efficacy based on some of the suggestions in this chapter.

REFERENCES

Bandura, A. (1977). Self-efficacy: Toward a unifying theory of behavioral change. *Psychological Review, 84*(2), 191–215.

Bandura, A. (1997). *Self-efficacy: The exercise of control.* New York: Freeman.

Bandura, A. (2012). On the functional properties of perceived self-efficacy revisited. *Journal of Management, 38*(1), 9–44.

Betoret, F. (2006). Stressors, self-efficacy, coping resources, and burnout among secondary school teachers in Spain. *Educational Psychology, 26*(4), 519–39

Boyd, E., & Fales, A. (1983). Reflective learning key to learning from experience. *Journal of Humanistic Psychology, 23*(2), 99–117.

Cashman, K. (2008). *Leadership from the inside out: Becoming a leader for life.* Provo, UT: Executive Excellence Publishing.

Council of Chief State School Officers (CCSSO). (2011). Interstate Teacher Assessment and Support Consortium (InTASC) model core teaching standards: A resource for state dialogue. Washington, DC.

Covey, S. (1989). *The seven habits of highly effective people.* New York, NY: Free Press.

Csikszentmihalyi, M. (1990). *Flow.* New York, NY: Harper & Row.

Dembo, M. H., & Gibson, S. (1985). Teachers' sense of efficacy: An important factor in school improvement. *The Elementary School Journal, 86*(2), 173–84.

Eggen, P., & Kauchak, D. (2001). *Educational psychology: Windows on classrooms.* Upper Saddle River, NJ: Prentice-Hall.

Evans, R. (2012). *Active strategies during inquiry-based science teacher education to improve long-term teacher self-efficacy.* Retrieved from http://www.esera.org/media/ebook/strand13/ebook-esera2011_EVANS-13.pdf.

Foote, C., Vermette, P., & Battaglia, C. (2001). *Constructivist strategies: Meeting standards and engaging adolescent minds.* Larchmont, NY: Eye on Education.

Holzberger, D., Philipp, A., & Kunter, M. (2013). How teachers' self-efficacy is related to instructional quality: A longitudinal analysis. *Journal of Educational Psychology, 105*(3), 774–86.

Hoy, A., & Spero, R. (2005). Changes in teacher efficacy during the early years of teaching: A comparison of four measures. *Teaching and Teacher Education, 21*(2005), 343–56.

Jennett, H., Harris, S., and Mesibov, G. (2003). Commitment to philosophy, teacher efficacy, and burnout among teachers of children with autism. *Journal of Autism and Developmental Disorders, 33*, 583–93.

Johnson, J., Collins, H., Duperes, V., & Johansen, J. (1991). *Foundations of American education.* Boston, MA: Allyn and Bacon.

Kelm, J., & McIntosh, K. (2012). Effects of school-wide positive behavior support on teacher self-efficacy. *Psychology in the Schools, 49*(2), 137–47.

Kobasa, S., Maddi, T., & Kahn, S. (1982). Hardiness and health: A prospective study. *Journal of Personality and Social Psychology, 42*(1), 168–77.

Litchka, P., Fenzel, M., & Polka, W. (2009). The stress process among school superintendents. *International Journal of Educational Leadership Preparation, 4*(4). Retrieved from http://ijelp.expressacademic.org.

Masunaga, H., & Lewis, T. (2011). Self-perceived dispositions that predict challenges during student teaching: A data mining analysis. *Issues in Teacher Education, 20*(1), 35–49.

Megginson, L. (1963). Lessons from Europe for American business. *Southwestern Social Science Quarterly, 44*(1), 3–13.

Olli-Pekke, M., Savolainen, H., Engelbrecht, P., Xu, J., Nel, M., Nel, N., & Tlale, D. (2013). Exploring teacher self-efficacy for inclusive practices in three diverse countries. *Teaching and Teacher Education, 33*, 34–44.

Ormond, J. (2006). *Educational Psychology: Developing learners* (5th ed.). Upper Saddle River, NJ: Pearson-Merrill Prentice-Hall.

Patterson, J. & Kelleher, P. (2005). *Resilient school leaders.* Alexandria, VA: Association for Supervision and Curriculum Development.

Polka, W. (1997). High-tech + high-touch = twenty-first century educational success. *Educational HORIZONS, 75*(2), 64–65.

Polka, W. (2010a). Facilitating instructional differentiation via teacher reflections about desired constructivist practices and current realities: A pragmatic research model. In E. Pultorak (Ed.), *The purposes, practices, and professionalism of teacher reflectivity: Insights for 21st century teachers and students* (pp. 163–88). New York, NY: Rowman & Littlefield.

Polka, W. (2010b). The art and science of constructivist supervision: Transforming schools by applying needs-based research. *Journal for the Practical Application of Constructivist Theory in Education, 5*(1), 1–28.

Polka, W., Pearman, C., and Bowles, F. (2011, February 15). Research paper on *Teacher self-efficacy: Findings from teacher educators at universities*. Presented at the Association of Teacher Educators National Conference.

Rabey, J. (2014). *The self-efficacy of New York State superintendents of schools and their self-reflective practices: A mixed-method analysis*. Unpublished doctoral dissertation, Niagara University.

Skaalvik, E., & Skaalvik, S. (2007). Dimensions of teacher self-efficacy and relations with strain factors, perceived collected teacher efficacy, and teacher burnout. *Journal of Educational Psychology, 99*(3), 611–35.

Skaalvik, E., & Skaalvik, S. (2010). Teacher self-efficacy and teacher burnout: A study of relations. *Teacher and Teacher Education, 26*, 1059–69.

Sternberg, R., & Williams, W. (2002). *Educational psychology.* Boston, MA: Houghton-Mifflin.

Chapter Seven

Curriculum as a Reflection of Teacher Self-Efficacy

Ashlie Jack, Kim McDowell, and Shirley LeFever

Alexis, a first-year, first-grade teacher, implored Ms. Groden, her mentor, "I get so frustrated by Jaden. He stares off into space and refuses to do the worksheets I pass out everyday. When I let him take them home, he returns them perfectly completed. His mom says he does his worksheets independently as soon as he gets home. I know he understands the material but he won't do the work in school.

"I have sent notes home trying to get his parents to make him behave in school but they say he is bored and says he doesn't think he should have to write his spelling words repeatedly. My district has a required curriculum that includes planned out lessons for every instructional unit I am supposed to teach for the year. My principal has told me I am required to use this curriculum. I feel so helpless."

After listening to Alexis describe her frustrations, Ms. Groden asked, "Can you tell me your overall goals for the academic year? What do you hope your students will learn or accomplish?" Alexis thought for a moment and replied, "I want to make sure they are reading and writing on grade level and they begin to develop some interests and understanding of basic curricular concepts."

"If you had no constraints on curriculum, what would you do to achieve this goal?" replied Ms. Groden. After pausing a few seconds, Alexis suggested, "I would engage them in learning activities that cause the students to think critically and create things." Ms. Groden then referred to a lesson Alexis would be teaching soon and asked, "Does this lesson do that? If not, what can you do to revise it so it works to accomplish your goals?"

America's future depends greatly on a high-quality teacher workforce. As articulated in the report of the National Commission on Teaching and America's Future (1996), there are three key premises for accomplishing this. First and foremost is the teacher's skill and knowledge base. The commission's report points out the clear relationship between student achievement and what teachers know and can do.

Further research (Lee, Patterson, & Vega, 2011) has identified teacher self-efficacy as a key aspect of teacher impact on student achievement. Teachers who believe they can have lasting effects on student achievement are more likely to approach curriculum design with a desire to engage learners in inquiry or problem-based learning. This chapter will explore issues related to teacher self-efficacy in regard to effective instructional models and will discuss the surrounding issues that teachers face as they develop their skills in this area.

A teacher's confidence in his or her ability to achieve long-reaching learning goals such as those described in the vignette above is directly related to a personal sense of self-efficacy (ibid.). Self-efficacious teachers realize the ability to plan and deliver instruction that is engaging for students will ultimately result in positive learning outcomes. However, not all teachers are self-efficacious. What makes one teacher more efficacious than another?

Researchers have indicated that self-efficacious behaviors result when early-career teachers experience success and recognize positive outcomes from their instruction (Hoy & Spero, 2005). In other words, success breeds success. Others (Elliott, Isaacs, & Chugani, 2010) add that early-career teachers need high-quality mentor programs that include feedback regarding instructional practices associated with positive student learning outcomes.

Such instructional practices are referenced in the Model Core InTASC Standards #7 and #8, which guide teachers to plan instruction designed to support every student in meeting rigorous learning goals and to use instructional strategies that promote student conceptual understandings and to develop skills that enable students to apply their knowledge in meaningful ways (CCSSO, 2011, p. 34).

EFFICACY DEFINED

In his seminal work, Bandura (1977) defined self-efficacy as "beliefs in one's capabilities to organize and execute the courses of action required to produce given attainments" (p. 3). Self-efficacy beliefs were characterized as the major mediators for our behavior, and importantly, behavioral change. Extant literature indicates that having a positive sense of efficacy is beneficial in many ways to teachers. "Teachers' beliefs in their personal efficacy to motivate and promote learning affect the types of learning environments they create and the level of academic progress their students achieve" (Bandura, 1993, p. 117).

Efficacious teachers believe they are self-empowered to create learning environments that allow them to motivate and promote student learning. Teachers' sense of teaching efficacy may impact their thoughts, choice of activities, amount of effort exerted, and extent of their persistence (Bandura, 1981). Allinder (1994) reported that efficacy is significantly related to instructionally relevant components of innovativeness in teaching, organization and planning of instruction, and confidence/enthusiasm. (McDowell et al., 2014).

WHY EFFICACY IS IMPORTANT

Founded in social cognitive theory, teachers' self-efficacy beliefs have been repeatedly associated with positive teaching behaviors and student outcomes. To be more specific, Lee, Patterson, & Vega (2011) examined personal teaching efficacy (PTE), which they defined as a teacher's confidence in "their ability to promote students' learning" (p. 62). PTE has been linked as a causal factor to (a) resiliency, (b) teacher effectiveness, (c) student achievement, and (d) the use of innovative teaching strategies.

Additionally, PTE has been shown to be correlated with (a) higher expectations and goals for students, (b) increased instructional time, and (c) more motivation for students. Tschannen-Moran & Woolfolk Hoy (2001) report that teachers' self-efficacy has been found to be related to: student achievement and motivation; students' efficacy beliefs; and teachers' efforts, persistence, resilience, willingness to try new methods, enthusiasm for teaching, commitment, and retention.

FACTORS THAT SUPPORT EFFICACY

Given that PTE is a valuable trait for teachers to possess, it is important to understand what factors are associated with having a high sense of PTE. Lee, Patterson, & Vega (2011) found several factors that were associated with having a high sense of PTE. These included the teaching context (e.g., availability of support and resources), confidence in knowledge and skills, and a sense of control/freedom.

Bandura (1986) argued that "perceived self-efficacy results from diverse sources of information conveyed vicariously and through social evaluation, as well as through direct experience" (p. 411). Finally, in a study conducted by Capa (2005), it was found that three factors statistically supported a new teacher's sense of efficacy. These include: teacher-preparation-program quality, principal support, and characteristics of the teaching assignment.

HOW EFFICACY DEVELOPS

Bandura (1986, 1977) proposed that there are four general sources of effica-cy-building information: verbal persuasion, vicarious experiences, physio-logical arousal, and mastery experiences. *Mastery experiences* involve direct opportunities for individuals to perform skills or actions. These experiences constitute the main source for shaping one's beliefs about self-efficacy. They provide authentic testimony about performance. A teacher's mastery experi-ence that results in negative consequences may lead to a decrease in efficacy.

Observing a model and vicarious experiences shapes one's own beliefs in self-efficacy in that one observes a model (mentor) performing a task and then reflects on the success and failures observed in comparison to one's own experience in the same situation. These experiences are influential in forming beliefs when the observed experience is on the level of the teacher's own abilities.

Social persuasion is the direct and indirect encouragement given to others through verbal messages and social encouragement. When given by a signifi-cant individual in the receiver's life, these messages help an individual to increase their efforts and aspire to additional successes. The greater the cred-ibility of the person, the larger the impact on the teacher's self-efficacy.

Physiological and/or affective responses are the physical symptoms of the body that are interpreted based on the individual's level of efficacy to the event or ability. When engaged in a task, one's increased state of anxiety or stress level can lower one's efficacy and feelings of failure. Of these, mastery experiences are likely the most powerful influence in fostering efficacy. Tschannen-Moran et al. (2001) also suggested that teacher efficacy actually is a joint, simultaneous function of a teacher's analysis of the teaching task and his or her assessment of his or her personal teaching competence or skill.

DEVELOPING SELF-EFFICACY AND THE EFFECTIVE TEACHER

During a time of reform and accountability across the nation, school districts are closely monitoring the instructional decisions, practices, and classroom environments of each teacher (Cassidy & Ortlieb, 2011). Teachers are striv-ing to make sense of the context of the policies governing the educational system as well as understand the required content standards, their assigned school site, and the demographics of their students.

In the midst of all of this turmoil, it is the teacher's confidence (efficacy) in their ability to promote student learning (Tschannen-Moran & Woolfolk Hoy, 2001) that allows for teacher success when striving to differentiate instruction. A level of self-efficacy must be developed through professional learning and mentoring programs that promote mastery experiences and self-reflection.

These experiences can strengthen one's self-efficacy through acquisition and mastery of knowledge and skills that can significantly impact student learning. It is high teacher self-efficacy that leads to learning environments that strive to overcome the bureaucracy of education, allowing one to create classrooms that meet the diverse learning needs of the gifted as well as the struggling learner yet at the same time meet the needs of the grade-level student.

PROFESSIONAL LEARNING

Professional learning (PL) presents a unique opportunity to immerse teachers in the essential work of the teaching profession (Mintzes et al., 2013). It is an opportunity for colleagues to engage in conversation to develop foundational understanding and instructional competencies for the topic at hand (Dixon et al., 2014) and for the social persuasion often needed to convince reluctant participants (Mintzes et al., 2013) to establish or implement effective practices resulting in positive student outcomes as reflected in InTASC Standards #7 and #8.

Professional learning is a productive way of engaging teachers in the kind of practice-based, action research that helps build a community of local scholars (Bilica, 2007). Teachers need ongoing and regular opportunities to learn from each other. This ongoing PL keeps teachers up-to-date on emerging technology tools for the classroom, new curriculum resources, and new research on how children learn (Mintzes et al., 2013). The best PL opportunities are ongoing, experiential, collaborative, and connected to and derived from working with students and understanding their culture.

Effective professional-learning opportunities introduce the topic and allow teachers the opportunity to practice the new knowledge in a "workshop" setting (Dixon et al., 2014). This type of setting allows teachers to work together coaching and supporting one another as they practice the new strategy through the designing of lessons and teaching assuring them of greater success in the classroom. This also gives educators the opportunity to collaborate on how the new strategy reflects the performances, essential knowledge, and critical dispositions within InTASC Standards #7 and #8.

The book *Standards for Professional Learning* (Learning Forward, 2011) established seven standards for professional learning to increase teacher effectiveness and results for all students. These standards outline the characteristics of professional learning that can lead to positive student outcome expectancies and contribute to the teachers' overall sense of self-efficacy and include the following:

1. Learning Communities: learning communities committed to continuous improvement, collective responsibility, and goal alignment;
2. Leadership: skillful leaders who develop capacity, advocate, and create support systems for professional learning;
3. Resources: prioritizing, monitoring, and coordinating resources for educator learning;
4. Data: use of a variety of sources and types of student, educator, and system data to plan, assess, and evaluate PL;
5. Learning Designs: integrates theories, research, and models of human learning to achieve its intended outcomes;
6. Implementation: applies research on change and sustains support for implementation of PL for long-term change; and
7. Outcomes: aligns outcomes with educator performance and student curricular standards.

MENTORING THROUGH MASTERY EXPERIENCES

Of the four general sources of efficacy-building information as proposed by Bandura (1986, 1977), mastery experiences are likely the most powerful influence in fostering self-efficacy. This source from which a person's feeling of efficacy grow can be enhanced through a strong mentoring program that fosters growth and success. These experiences allow a teacher to perform skills or actions for their mentor and receive authentic feedback about their performance in regard to planning for instruction and the implementation of instructional strategies (InTASC Standards #7 and #8).

Mentoring has been defined as "a relationship between an experienced and a less experienced person in which the mentor provides guidance, advice, support and feedback to a protégé" (Kerka, 1998, p. 3). While teacher education has long adopted the apprenticeship model in mentoring, mentoring includes emotional support and professional socialization in addition to pedagogical guidance (Hawkey, 2006; Schwille, 2008). Mentoring of early-career teachers that results in truly skilled professionals requires continued support and supervision in improving self-efficacy for teaching and in managing large class sizes, standardized testing, and a mandated curriculum.

A strong mentoring program promotes a supportive and instructive environment in which early-career teachers can continue to develop professionally, which in turn can increase teacher effectiveness. Teacher effectiveness is generally characterized as improving student learning and may be one of the most important factors contributing to students' academic achievement (Wright, Horn, & Sanders, 1997). Elliott, Isaacs & Chugani (2010) suggest the following initial strategies to utilize in promoting early-career teacher self-efficacy, quality of teaching, and retention through a strong mentoring program.

- *Do not make the first year of teaching a game of "education survivor."* Early-career teachers need constant support and supervision in order to feel improvement in their confidence levels.
- *Set a good example by providing individualized attention.* Principals and building administrators should get to know their new teachers, understand their learning styles and their individual needs, and provide individualized support to maximize the teacher's self-efficacy.
- *Assess early-career teacher self-efficacy and learning needs.* Individual teachers need to be assessed in key areas of competence (e.g., teaching ESOL students and students who have learning disabilities and using standardized test results to modify instruction and behavior management) through self-reporting and observation.
- *Have "quick strategies" available.* Limit the amount of time during which the teacher experiences low levels of confidence by having specific plans or methods (e.g., DVD/video, written step-by-step processes, and/or research) in place to address teacher concerns in key areas of competence. This approach sends the message that such concerns may be normal for early-career teachers and breaks problems down into smaller, more manageable pieces, which can increase confidence/self-efficacy.
- *Match mentors' strengths with new teachers' needs.* Deliberately match early-career teachers with mentors who are skilled in addressing the specific individual's area of need. Avoid assigning mentors based solely on number of years in the field and/or willingness to serve.
- *Conduct targeted observation, and provide timely feedback.* Assigned mentors and principals should observe for targeted skills only and (1) provide quick feedback; (2) schedule additional observation to ensure progress; and (3) break down necessary priorities, knowledge, and/or skills into manageable pieces and/or realistic timelines to promote effective and efficient problem solving.
- *Develop building-level mentoring programs and/or join with a partner school to provide mentor exchanges.* Develop an on-site mentoring program that promotes a supportive and instructive environment in which early-career teachers can continue to develop professionally, or create a partnership with another school to introduce more targeted strengths where needed.
- *Get other teachers in the building invested in the success of new teachers.* An established set of incentives can create an environment that promotes collaboration and professional growth between new-career and veteran teachers. Teachers already established in the profession need to feel appreciated for their efforts in improving education and have the opportunity to

professionally grow through incentives such as professional development, training opportunities for working with new teachers, or a gift of professional classroom materials and/or technology.

- *Adapt a quick questionnaire to target specific competencies.* Utilize a questionnaire (developed by the building principal or a checklist developed from the state's or district's identified key teacher competencies) as a preliminary guide to determine professional development and observation activities for early-career and veteran teachers.
- *Track effective practices within districts.* Determine the best induction programs and mentoring practices by other districts that have maintained a higher retention rate of their teachers.

SELF-REFLECTION

Howe (2006) suggests that a key element in successful teacher induction is the provision of time for reflection. Bandura (1986) considered self-reflection an important personal attribute that contributes to one's ability to positively alter one's own thinking and behavior: thinking and behavior in regard to planning instruction based on formative and summative assessment data, the use of appropriate strategies and resources, adapting the instruction to meet the needs of the learners, and the engagement of all learners through higher level questioning and metacognition (InTASC Standards #7 and #8).

Grimmett, Erickson, Mackinnon, & Riecken (1990) proposed four modes of thinking empowering teachers to connect reflection to practical classroom applications. When used appropriately, these modes of critical reflection allow a teacher to evaluate the efficacy of their own practice and determine whether their teaching practices foster accomplished teaching and impact student learning. They include the following:

1. technological thinking—reflective thinking that relies on practices that have proven efficient and effective as an external source to make decisions about teaching practices in place;
2. situational thinking—a quick reflection with immediate response focused only on information embedded in a specific context at a specific time such as the observation of student behavior at that moment;
3. deliberate thinking—purposefully seeking more information for the immediate context through thoughtful reflection; and
4. dialectical thinking—a mode of reflection that builds on deliberate thinking to increase understanding of a situation and generate solutions.

FINAL THOUGHTS

Research by Hoy & Spero (2005) concludes that the development of teachers' self-efficacy is most important in the very early phases of teacher induction and argues that strategies geared toward this goal will be most effective when focused on mastery experiences. In other words, when teachers feel their instruction has resulted in increased student learning, they have a tendency to believe future attempts at instruction will also produce positive results.

Hoy and Spero also found early career teachers' sense of efficacy is impacted by the support they receive. This finding is further reinforced by Elliott, Isaacs, and Chugani (2010), who argue for differentiated mentoring and supervision of early-career teachers.

REFLECTION

A well-established sense of efficacy has been positively correlated with student achievement and teacher retention. Given this, there is a strong need to promote teacher self-efficacy. Chief among the strategies to promote early-career teachers' self-efficacy is professional learning that engages teachers in the kind of practice-based, action research that helps build a community of local scholars, a comprehensive approach to mentoring that fosters growth and success through Bandura's contributors to the development of self-efficacy, and time for self-reflection practices in order to foster accomplished teaching and impact student learning

DISCUSSION QUESTIONS

1. After reading the opening vignette, reflect on the sources of frustration being exhibited by Jaden, his parents, and the teacher. What needs are being met or overlooked by each person?
2. Reflect on Alexis's goals for the year she described in the opening vignette. Are they appropriate? How might her perception of the curriculum be prohibiting her from meeting these goals and contributing to Jaden's lack of engagement?
3. What is your perception of the curriculum in your district? Is it prohibiting or enhancing your ability to meet the academic needs of your students?
4. How do you apply your professional learning to your classroom to enhance student learning and your sense of self-efficacy?
5. How is mentoring implemented in your school and/or district to promote a supportive and instructional learning environment?

6. How do you utilize critical reflection to evaluate the efficacy of your own practices and ensure your practices foster accomplished teaching and impact student learning?

RESOURCES

1. *Professional Learning Resources*: Professional learning opportunities should be designed to develop knowledge, skills, and behaviors to improve teacher practice and effectiveness leading to increased student achievement. http://learningforward.org/ and http://www.nysteachercenters.org/resources/professional-learning-resources/.

2. *Mentoring-New Teacher Center*: One such national model for developing a strong mentoring program is the nationally recognized New Teacher Center (NTC). www.newteachercenter.org. The NTC asserts mentor-based support programs foster retention and transform learning communities.

3. *Mentor Resources*: A district and/or school can design their own quality mentoring program by utilizing this comprehensive set of materials. http://www.neafoundation.org/downloads/NEA-Creating_Teacher_Mentoring.pdf.

4. *Self-Reflection*. Reflection can begin by asking yourself questions such as the ones found at this link: http://teachnet.com/how-to/organization/092998.html.

REFERENCES

Allinder, R. M. (1994). The relationship between efficacy and the instructional practices of special education teachers and consultants. *Teacher Education and Special Education, 17,* 86–95.

Bandura, A. (1977). Self-Efficacy: Toward a unifying theory of behavioral change. *Psychological Review, 84*(2), 191–215.

Bandura, A. (1981). Self-referent thought: *A* developmental analysis of self-efficacy. In J. H. Flavell and L. Ross (Eds.), *Social cognitive development; Frontiers and possible futures.* Cambridge: Cambridge University Press.

Bandura, A. (1986). *Social foundations of thought and action: A social cognitive theory.* Englewood Cliffs, NJ: Prentice-Hall.

Bandura, A. (1993). Perceived self-efficacy in cognitive development and functioning. *Educational Psychologist, 28*(2) 117–48.

Bilica, K. (2007). Taking action in elementary science teaching: A reflection on four teachers' collaborative research journey. *Networks, An Online Journal for Teacher Research, 9*(1), 1–10.

Capa, Y. (2005). *Factors influencing first year teachers' sense of efficacy.* Unpublished doctoral dissertation. Ohio State University, Columbus.

Cassidy, J., & Ortlieb, E. (2011). Literacy—The first decade of the new millennium. *Reading Horizons, 51*(2), 93–102.

Council of Chief State School Officers (CCSSO). (2011). Interstate teacher assessment and support consortium (InTASC) model core teaching standards: A resource for state dialogue. *Council of Chief State School Officers.* Washington, DC: Retrieved from http://www.ccsso.org/documents/2011/intasc_model_core_teaching_standards_2011.pdf.

Dixon, F. A., Yssel, N., McConnell, J. M., & Hardin, T. (2014). Differentiated instruction professional development, and teacher efficacy. *Journal for the Education of the Gifted, 37*(2), 111–27.

Elliott, E. M., Isaacs, M. L., & Chugani, C. D., (2010). Promoting self-efficacy in early career teachers: A principal's guide for differentiated mentoring and supervision. *Florida Journal of Educational Administration & Policy, 4*(1), 131–46.

Grimmet, P. P., Erickson, G. L., Mackinnon, A. A., & Riecken, T. J. (1990). Reflective practice in teacher education. In R. T. Clift, W. R. Houston, and M. C. Pugach (Eds.), *Encouraging reflective practice in education: An analysis of issues and programs* (pp. 20–38). New York, NY: Teachers College Press.

Hawkey, K. (2006). Emotional intelligence and mentoring in pre-service teacher education: A literature review. *Mentoring & Tutoring: Partnership in Learning, 14*(2), 137–47.

Howe, E. R. (2006). Exemplary teacher induction: An international review. *Educational Philosophy and Theory, 38*(3), 287–97.

Hoy, A. W., & Spero, R. B., (2005). Changes in teacher efficacy during the early years of teaching: A comparison of four measures. *Teaching and Teacher Education, 21*, 343–56.

Johnson, S. (2009). *Comprehensive induction or add-on induction: Impact on teacher practice and student engagement.* New Teacher Center Research Brief. Santa Cruz, CA: Retrieved from http://www.newteachercenter.org/sites/default/files/ntc/main/resources/BRF_ ComprehensiveInductionorAdd-onInduction.pdf.

Kerka, S. (1998). *New perspectives on mentoring. ERIC Clearinghouse on Adult Career and Vocational Education.* Retrieved November 18, 2006 from http://www.guidancechannel. com/default.aspx?M=a&index=1103&cat=9.

Learning Forward (2011). *Standards for Professional Learning.* Oxford, OH. Retrieved from http://learningforward.org/standards-for-professional-learning#.VMKOSU0tG72.

Lee, Y., Patterson, P. P., & Vega, L. (2011, Spring). Perils to self-efficacy perceptions and teacher-preparation quality among special education intern teachers. *Teacher Education Quarterly*, 61–76.

McDowell, K., Jack, A., Carroll, J., & Ewing, J. (2014). Preservice and novice teacher self-efficacy: A tool to understand and further develop confidence for impacting change. *The Advocate, 22*(1), 43–49.

Mintzes, J. J., Marcum, B., Messerschmidt-Yates, C., & Mark, A. (2013). Enhancing self-efficacy in elementary science teaching with professional learning communities. *Journal of Science Teacher Education, 24*, 1201–18.

National Commission on Teaching and America's Future. (1996). *What Matters Most: Teaching for America's Future.* New York, NY: Author.

Roberts, A. (2013). STEM is here. Now what? *Technology and Engineering Teacher, 37*(1), 22–27.

Schwille, S. A. (2008). The professional practice of mentoring. *American Journal of Education, 115*(1), 139–67.

Tschannen-Moran, M., & Woolfolk Hoy, A. (2001). Teacher-efficacy: Capturing an elusive construct. *Teaching and Teacher Education, 17*, 783–805.

Wright, S. P., Horn, S. P., & Sanders, W. L. (1997). Teacher and classroom context effects on student achievement: Implications for teacher evaluation. *Journal of Personnel Evaluation in Education, 11*, 57–67. Retrieved from http://www.sas.com/govedu/edu/teacher_eval.pdf.

Chapter Eight

Control and Self-Efficacy

Terrell M. Peace

Carol, a veteran elementary teacher with fifteen years of experience and a master's degree in curriculum and instruction was having Saturday morning coffee with her friend and fellow teacher, Michelle. The two often get together to discuss their teaching experiences. As is often the case with teachers for the last several years, the conversation turns to the impact that federal regulations and standardized testing have had on classrooms and learning.

> ***Carol****: Sometimes I feel like a marionette, going through the motions of teaching, with No Child Left Behind, Race to the Top, Common Core, and standardized testing pulling the strings to make me dance this meaningless, data-crazed ballet that both my experience and my knowledge of teaching and learning tell me is not what is best for my kids. I want to move back toward a broad curriculum and differentiated instruction to give my students what they really need, but the puppet masters are constantly pulling me in the other direction, using the specter of teacher evaluations to force compliance.*
>
> ***Michelle****: I know exactly what you mean! I was going through my files a couple of weeks ago and ran across some of my favorite science lessons, and my immediate thought was, "Why haven't I used these lately? The kids always got so much out of them because the learning is so active." Then I remembered, I hardly ever get to teach science anymore, since it is not tested on the state assessments.*
>
> ***Carol****: I can't even remember the last time I had a hands-on science lesson, not to mention social studies. Do you remember all those great activities for teaching civics and citizenship that we learned in our teacher preparation program? I know that math and language arts are important, but what happened to trusting teachers and schools to give students what they need, when they need it?*
>
> ***Michelle****: Carol, I hate to admit it, but I have so little control over what happens in my classroom now that I am beginning to wonder if I was ever as competent as I thought I was. I hate having these doubts about myself and my*

abilities. I have even been thinking seriously about quitting teaching and doing something where I can feel like I have more control over my own destiny.
Carol: *I understand completely! When I made the decisions about what to teach and how to teach it and implemented lessons in the ways that I was trained to do, I felt like I could help any student learn. I felt like I was a professional and a guiding influence in my classroom. Now, I am not so sure that I am making much of a difference in any student's life.*

Self-Efficacy: The Exercise of Control, the seminal work by Bandura (1997), established a solid basis for connections between the characteristics of control and self-efficacy. In the twenty-first-century classroom, the connections between teacher self-efficacy and the issues related to control are complex and multidimensional. In the pages to follow, we will explore the relationship between teacher control and teacher self-efficacy and what that means for teachers, students, and learning.

INTERNAL OR EXTERNAL CONTROL

Locus of control (Rotter, 1966) describes what we believe about the extent to which we determine outcomes of our own performance or whether we believe those outcomes are determined by external forces that are beyond our control. "Individuals with an internal locus of control are more likely to believe that they have the ability to influence their work context and are therefore more likely to feel empowered than individuals with an external locus of control" (Wang, Zhang, & Jackson, 2013, p. 1428).

Persons with an internal locus of control feel empowered in their work context more often than those with an external locus of control (Luo and Tang, 2003). And, in fact, Wang, Zhang, and Jackson (2013) in their research found that "internal locus of control was positively associated with all subscales of psychological empowerment" (p. 1431). Those with an internal locus of control feel they have more control of and responsibility for their own life situations.

Based on Bandura's (1997) descriptions of self-efficacy, Skaalvik and Skaalvik (2007) say that "teacher self-efficacy may be conceptualized as individual teacher's beliefs in their own abilities to plan, organize, and carry out activities required to attain given educational goals" (p. 612). Teachers who have this belief in their own ability to teach effectively and exhibit a strong sense of self-efficacy have been found to worry less about the demands of teaching and about their own continuation as teachers (Ghaith & Shaaban, 1999).

As a result, these teachers are more willing to take the risks associated with innovative practices aimed at meeting a wide variety of educational needs (Wertheim & Leyser, 2002) and "are able to bring about more effective learning and able to motivate and meet the learning needs of their students while being less likely to blame themselves for poor student learning outcomes" (Ng, Nicholas, & Williams, 2010, p. 279).

HIGH-STAKES TESTING AND THE NARROWING OF THE CURRICULUM

Both Carol and Michelle in the opening vignette lamented the narrowing of the curriculum that has occurred over the past few years. The now iconic No Child Left Behind (NCLB) legislation required that all students be proficient in reading and mathematics by 2014, and states were required to test in those two subjects in order to prove that the demands were being met. Because of the high stakes for schools related to meeting NCLB standards, more time was given in the school day for teaching, practicing, and testing in mathematics and reading, and consequently less time was given to other subjects.

Ravitch (2013) stated, "This unnatural focus on testing produced perverse but predictable results: it narrowed the curriculum; many districts scaled back time for the arts, history, civics, physical education, science, foreign language, and whatever was not tested" (p. 13). Shea and Ceprano (2013) conclude that further narrowing of the curriculum has occurred because the agenda of high-stakes testing has resulted in the promotion of scripted programs such as Reading First, Open Court, and Direct Instruction that ignore the cultural, language, and economic differences which must be addressed in twenty-first-century classrooms.

When competition for school funds was tied to school performance by Secretary of Education Arne Duncan in the Race to the Top (RTT) legislation, states were compelled:

> to adopt new common standards and tests (the Common Core State Standards); expand the number of charter schools; evaluate the effectiveness of teachers in significant part by the test scores of their students (and remove any statutory barriers to doing so); and agree to "turn around" their lowest-performing schools by taking such dramatic steps as firing staff and closing schools. (Ravitch, 2013, p. 14)

The double-barreled threat of NCLB-based school closings and RTT teacher evaluations, both based largely on standardized test scores for math and reading/language arts, has put further pressure on schools and teachers to abandon a normal curriculum and focus exclusively on what is tested on state tests. This pressure in the educational setting requires teachers to have a high degree of self-efficacy and a strong internal locus of control to adapt to and successfully negotiate these requirements.

While the impact of the narrowed curriculum was felt initially in elementary classrooms, Thomas Poetter (2013) points out that teachers at all levels are now struggling to regain control of the curriculum and teaching in their own classrooms.

> In fact, high school teachers who enjoyed freedom from the mandate of the high-stakes testing regime are now being chased, pursued, and finally hobbled by the standardization movement. Ultimately, the results are a not-so-subtle narrowing of the curriculum and the pedagogy of the classroom teacher. (p.102)

A teacher survey conducted by researchers at the University of North Carolina at Chapel Hill asked teachers to identify what they needed to be successful as teachers. The survey was active for over eight years and represented a broad range of teachers, over half of whom were National Board Certified (Dagenhart et al., 2005). "Regarding the top professional development needs, teachers wanted and needed direct, practical teaching experiences in the classroom and more control over the curriculum, instructional methods, topics, and time" (ibid., p. 109).

Teachers understand that the forced narrowing of the curriculum, especially the use of scripted programs, implies that they do not have the knowledge necessary to make appropriate curricular and pedagogical decisions and takes away the empowerment of being able to use their own professional expertise (Shea & Ceprano, 2013). Stallions, Murrill, & Earp (2012) identify the frustration felt by teachers at the lack of control in making curricular decisions as a factor leading to "self-doubt and an unsteady sense of professional efficacy" (p. 127), feelings that are linked to thoughts about leaving the teaching profession.

CLOSING THOUGHTS

So what if a teacher's self-efficacy is related to a sense of control over elements in his or her classroom? So what if a teacher's sense of control is negatively impacted by the narrowing of the curriculum? So what if the loss of control has resulted in decreased teacher efficacy for classroom teachers in the twenty-first century? These connections are strategically important because there is a direct, well-established relationship between teacher self-efficacy and student achievement (Bandura, 1993; Goddard, Hoy, & Woolfolk Hoy, 2000; Woolfolk Hoy, Hoy, & Davis, 2009; Guo et al., 2010). In summation of her research (Woolfolk Hoy, Hoy, & Davis, 2009), Anita Woolfolk says:

Teachers with higher efficacy judgments tend to be more open to new ideas; more willing to experiment with new methods to better meet the needs of their students; more likely to use powerful but potentially difficult-to-manage methods such as inquiry and small-group work; and less likely to use easy-to-adopt but weaker methods such as lectures. Higher efficacy teachers are less likely to criticize students and more persistent in following up on incorrect student answers. (Woolfolk, 2013, p. 409)

So, there it is. If we want higher student achievement, then we must return the control and professional autonomy that has been taken from classroom teachers in the NCLB and RTT era. Effective teachers are efficacious teachers.

DISCUSSION QUESTIONS

1. In what ways did the conversation between Carol and Michelle in the opening vignette reflect the issues discussed in the paragraphs above on locus of control and teacher efficacy?
2. InTASC Standard #9 indicates that teachers should be reflective practitioners who evaluate the effect of their choices on others. How can teachers regain a sense of control when so many of the choices they implement are made by external entities?
3. Describe how each of the three teacher abilities identified in Skaalvik and Skaalvik's definition of teacher self-efficacy is impacted by a teacher's loss of professional autonomy in the classroom.
4. How has the narrowing of the curriculum associated with standardized testing and the inclusion of more designated teaching strategies as part of the Common Core Curriculum made teachers feel about the control they exert in the classroom?
5. How did Carol and Michelle express the impact of the narrowed curriculum on their own feelings of control and their teacher efficacy?
6. How has the climate in the test-score-centered classroom in the NCLB and RTT era impacted teacher control, self-efficacy, and by extension, student achievement?
7. How has the implementation of cryptic, data-based evaluation systems of teacher competency impacted the classroom teacher's sense of control?
8. Why does it make sense that there would be a positive correlation between teacher self-efficacy and persistence with hard-to-reach students or hard-to-teach subjects?
9. How would you explain the relationship between teacher efficacy and student achievement?

10. Explain the difference between a teacher's personal self-efficacy and his or her teacher self-efficacy. Which do you think is more important and why?

REFERENCES

Bandura, A. (1993). Perceived self-efficacy in cognitive development and functioning. *Educational Psychologist, 28*(2), 117–48.

Bandura, A. (1997). *Self-Efficacy: The exercise of control.* New York, NY: Academic Press.

Dagenhart, D., O'Connor, K., Petty, T., & Day, B. (2005). Giving teachers a voice. *Kappa Delta Pi Record, 41*(3), 108–11.

Ghaith, G., & Shaaban, K. (1999). The relationship between conceptions of teacher concerns, teacher efficacy, and selected teacher characteristics. *Teaching and Teacher Education, 15*(5), 487–96.

Goddard, R., Hoy, W., & Woolfolk Hoy, A. (2000). Collective teacher efficacy: Its meaning, measure, and impact on student achievement. *American Educational Research Journal, 37,* 479–508.

Guo, Y., Piasta, S., Justice, L., & Kaderavek, J. (2010). Relations among preschool teachers' self-efficacy, classroom quality, and children's language and literacy gains. *Teaching and Teacher Education, 26,* 1094–1103.

Luo, S., & Tang, Y. (2003). The effects of internal-external personality trait and empowerment on job satisfaction—based on a sample of insurance company employees. *Journal of Human Resource Management, 3,* 1–19.

Ng, W., Nicholas, H., & Williams, A. (2010). School experience influences on pre-service teachers' evolving beliefs about effective teaching. *Teaching and Teacher Education, 26,* 278–89.

Poetter, T. (2013). Stemming the tide: Calvin's high-water mark and teacher resistance. *Kappa Delta Pi Record, 49*(3), 100–104.

Ravitch, D. (2013). *Reign of error: The hoax of the privatization movement and the danger to America's public schools.* New York, NY: Alfred A. Knopf.

Rotter, J. B. (1966). Generalized expectancies for internal versus external control of reinforcement. *Psychological Monographs, 80,* 1–28.

Shea, M., & Ceprano, M. (2013). The attack on teachers and schools of education: Identifying the bullies and bystanders. *Kappa Delta Pi Record, 49*(1), 4–8.

Skaalvik, E., & Skaalvik, S. (2007). Dimensions of teacher self-efficacy and relations with strain factors, perceived collective teacher efficacy, and teacher burnout. *Journal of Educational Psychology, 99*(3), 611–25.

Stallions, M., Murrill, L., & Earp, L. (2012). Don't quit now!: Crisis, reflection, growth, and renewal for early career teachers. *Kappa Delta Pi Record, 48*(3), 123–28.

Wertheim, C. & Leyser, Y. (2002). Efficacy beliefs, background variables, and differentiated instruction of Israeli prospective teachers. *The Journal of Educational Research, 96,* 54–63.

Woolfolk, A., (2013). *Educational psychology* (12th ed.). Boston, MA: Pearson.

Woolfolk Hoy, A., Hoy, W. K., and Davis, H., (2009). Teachers' self-efficacy beliefs. In K. Wentzel & A. Wigfield (Eds.), *Handbook of motivation in school.* Mahwah, NJ: Erlbaum.

Chapter Nine

On the Culture of Collaboration

A Tool for Teacher Self-Efficacy

Jennifer Beasley

I am not quite sure how, but suddenly I feel like I am a real member of the school community. I feel as though I know what I am doing, I'm confident in my role, and I finally feel like I am doing a good job! The other day I was having a conversation with someone who asked me if I was a teacher at Eagle Elementary. I replied, "I'm actually an intern." So, not a real teacher, but still learning how to be a teacher. Ms. C happened to be listening to the conversation and added, "Now, don't let her tell you she's not a real teacher. She is still in school, but all the kindergarten teachers consider her to be just as much a teacher as the rest of us."

This statement meant so much to me and I really appreciated Ms. C adding that to the conversation. It made me feel like I really am a part of the kindergarten team, and it was awesome to be included. Although this seems like a somewhat insignificant incident, it has been a highlight as of recently (Linda, teacher candidate).

Feeling a part of a community is one of the cornerstones for impacting confidence for a teacher (Hattie, 2012). Goddard et al. (2000) supported the relationship between community and individual by positing that when individual teacher efficacy is improved, the entire culture of the organization improves. As for Linda, her short hallway conversation with an experienced teacher in her school promoted her self-efficacy, which is defined as a belief in one's capability to plan and carry out change (Bandura, 1977; Hoy, 2000).

Given the rapid increase in students with diverse needs in public schools, are there partnerships that universities can support that might promote the kind of collaboration that leads to enhanced teacher efficacy? In this study, one mid-south university was looking at whether the partnerships they developed within the university and neighboring school districts had an impact on teacher practices and efficacy in meeting the needs of students.

THEORETICAL FRAMEWORK

The landscape of the classroom is changing. Over the last ten years, information from the IDEA Data Accountability Center (http://www.ideadata.org) indicates the number of U.S. students with disabilities enrolled in special education programs has risen 30 percent. Three out of every four of these students spend part or all of their school day in general education classrooms.

Despite this increase in learners with special learning needs as well as the increase in culturally and linguistically diverse (CLD) students, there is little evidence to suggest that most teachers are adjusting their instruction in ways that would support a full range of students (Moon, Tomlinson, & Callahan, 1995; Westberg et al., 1993; Westberg & Daoust, 2003). The reality of teacher candidates facing diverse classrooms without the pedagogical skills to tailor instruction for the needs of learners is an inherent need every teacher candidate program faces each year (Darling-Hammond & Leiberman, 2012; Goodwin et al., 2014).

Teacher educators can draw on powerful learning communities both within and without formal schools of education to support teacher candidates (Goodwin et al., 2014) and enhance their professional learning community. Guiding teacher candidates to access the expertise found through the learning community not only makes good sense but also exemplifies InTASC Standard #9: "engages in ongoing professional learning . . . and adapts practice to meet the needs of each learner" (CCSSO, 2011).

Building on the literature of teacher efficacy and partnerships, one university system sought to explore the impact of collaboration within and among the university and partnership school settings on teachers.

Teacher Efficacy

Teacher efficacy is defined as the confidence a teacher has in the ability to promote student achievement. Bandura (1977; 1997) cited three primary influences on efficacy: mastery experiences, vicarious experiences, and social persuasion. With mastery experience, the teacher sees that his or her performance has been successful. With vicarious experience, the teacher sees someone else model a skill that has resulted in success. Finally, with social persuasion, a teacher receives a "pep talk" from a supervisor or colleague that encourages her or him to try a new skill or strategy in the classroom.

Some of the most powerful influences on the development of teacher efficacy early in a teacher's career are mastery experiences during student teaching and the induction year (Hoy & Spero, 2005; Mulholland & Wallace,

2001). In addition, efficacy judgments are most malleable in the early stages to mastering a skill. It makes sense that early teaching experiences would be important shapers of efficacy judgments (Woolfolk Hoy, 2003–2004).

Encouraging partnerships, such as mentoring, can provide opportunities for vicarious experiences as well as social persuasion that may contribute to a boost in self-efficacy, which in turn may lead to someone initiating a task, attempting a new strategy, or trying hard enough to succeed (Bandura, 1982).

Partnerships

Partnerships, as defined in this study, have their naissance in the work of the Holmes Partnership. The Holmes Partnership began in response to some disturbing reform trends cited in *A Nation at Risk* (1983) such as (a) a number of the nation's strongest universities' elimination of their schools of education; (b) these same universities' beliefs that schools of education could be entrusted to universities of lesser rank; and (c) a general view that education schools had not lived up to their potential, nor would they in the future (Holmes Group, 1986).

The Holmes Partnership was formed as a collaborative partnership between public schools and universities whose goal was to improve the quality of teacher education. The Holmes Partnership posited that when practicing teachers, teacher candidates, and university faculty work together through the provision of high-quality, field-based educational experiences, public education is improved through the sharing of resources and enhancement of teacher preparation (Holmes Group, 1995).

A collaborative partnership is designed to achieve clearly defined, mutually agreed upon goals (ibid.). In studies where teachers were allowed to participate in a community of practice, new teacher learning was observed and efficacy increased (Kennedy & Smith, 2013). Collaborative partnerships have existed between the university in this study and one school district in the mid-south since 1992.

This partnership moved beyond formal university/school partnerships, such as the student teaching experience, to include informal partnerships where university faculty were welcome in the schools as visitors, researchers, and providers of information on new teaching strategies and research-based instructional models.

RESEARCH STUDY CONTEXT

Many universities and teacher colleges offer preparation on meeting the needs of diverse learners to both pre-service and in-service teachers. Formal preparation includes coursework leading to an endorsement, an additional license plan, or a standard license. Professional development on meeting the needs of students of other cultures and those with a primary language other than English for pre-service teachers and for teachers already licensed in a standard area comprises the curriculum for an endorsement in English as a second language (ESL).

Professional development for pre-service teachers and for teachers already licensed in a standard area on meeting the needs of students with disabilities comprises a curriculum for a license in special education (SPED). However, in the mid-south, one school district provides professional development for such credentialing through a variety of formal and informal partnerships.

Through the university and school district partnership, pre-service educators are provided school-based field experiences to obtain more training in meeting the needs of diverse students. Pre-service teachers obtaining an elementary teaching license may choose between an additional endorsement in ESL or a license in SPED.

In addition to more formal collaboration at the university level, the university sponsors symposia (literacy, autism, and ESL) and in-service training to the school district personnel in partnership with surrounding school districts. Teachers use these professional-development activities to expand their professional skill repertoire and meet the professional-development standards required for license renewal. It is through these partnerships that schools and teacher-education programs can support the basic tenets of the Holmes Partnership (Holmes Group, 1995).

METHODOLOGY

In this study, the researchers looked at the beliefs and reported practice in meeting the needs of diverse learners of elementary teachers in one school district served by university partnerships in one mid-south community. Research questions that drove this study were: What is the impact of the explicit training to meet the needs of diverse students, once teachers are placed in the field? What is the role of partnership schools as well as teacher education programs to inform teacher efficacy?

Participants

This quantitative study involved 139 teachers from eight elementary schools purposefully selected from one school district in the mid-south. Of the teachers surveyed, 59 percent of them graduated from the university where the partnership programs were offered. The school district serves students from pre-kindergarten through grade twelve. The district in which the schools were selected has a total of 18,810 students in twenty-six schools.

The ethnic breakdown for the school district is as follows: 43 percent white; 43 percent Hispanic; 8 percent Native Hawaiian/Pacific Islander; 3 percent African American; 2 percent Asian; and less than 1 percent Native American/Native Alaskan. Students identified as limited-English-proficient make up 43 percent of the district population, whereas 38 percent are general education, 10 percent are in the gifted and talented program, and 9 percent are in the district's special education program. The district serves 12,039 students who are eligible for the free and reduced lunch program, which is approximately 64 percent of the district population.

Data Collection

The Elementary Teacher Survey used in this study was a modification of a survey previously used in a nationwide sample of middle school teachers (Moon, Tomlinson, & Callahan, 1995), along with a modification of the short form of the teacher self-efficacy scale (Hoy & Spero, 2005). The survey was developed to reflect the beliefs and practices of elementary teachers in relation to serving their student population.

Practices and conditions investigated included beliefs about how students learn, arrangement of students for learning, cooperative learning, acknowledging and dealing with student differences, and curriculum, instruction, and assessment practices. The survey offered statements that were rated on a Likert-type scale with anchors from *strongly believe* to *do not believe at all* or *reflects my everyday practice* to *never a part of my classroom* (Figure 9.1).

Participation in the study was voluntary, and all participants were informed that all information would be kept confidential and that the results would only be reported in statistical form so as not to identify any individual responses.

RESULTS

Teachers in this study related information having to do with their beliefs and practices in serving the needs of diverse students. Specifically, information was collected about (a) how much their instructional practice is shaped by student needs, (b) the reported use of instructional strategies with diverse students, (c) feelings of self-efficacy when meeting the needs of students, and (d) beliefs about differentiating instruction.

Student Influence on Instructional Practice

The teachers were asked to rate how much their own instructional practice was shaped by the academic needs of culturally diverse students, limited English proficient students, learners with disabilities, and advanced/gifted

For question 1, we ask you to RATE each item according to the degree to which the needs of the group influence your instructional planning and practice. In rating each item please use the following scale:

No Influence=1
Rarely Influences=2
Somewhat Influences=3
Strongly Influences=4
Dominates=5

1. How much of your instructional practice is shaped by the academic needs of each of the following groups?

	no influence	rarely influences	some influence	strong influence	dominates
a. Culturally diverse learners	1	2	3	4	5
b. Remedial learners	1	2	3	4	5
c. ELL/Bilingual learners	1	2	3	4	5
d. Advanced/gifted learners	1	2	3	4	5
e. Learners with disabilities	1	2	3	4	5
f. Average learners	1	2	3	4	5
g. Consideration of the whole class as a single unit	1	2	3	4	5

Figure 9.1.

students (Figure 9.1). The teachers used the scale *no influence, rarely influences, some influence, strong influence, and dominates* to rate the influence on their practice.

Studies have noted that teachers who are more efficacious are more willing to readily adjust instruction for their students (Goddard et al., 2000; Hattie, 2012). This indicator revealed that all of the student groups were reported to have some influence on teachers' instructional practices, with bilingual and culturally diverse learners having the strongest influence (81 percent and 76 percent, respectively). The student group with the least influence on instructional practice was reported to be advanced/gifted learners (47 percent).

Reported Use of Instructional Strategies

Teachers were asked how often certain instructional activities were used in their classrooms with English language learners (ELLs) and learners with

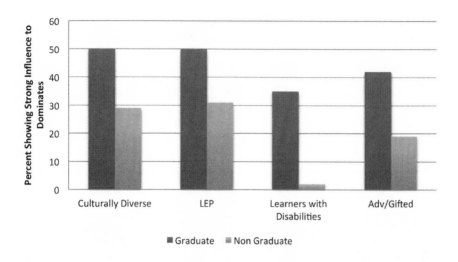

Figure 9.2.

disabilities (LD). With ELL, graphic organizers, pre-assessment, and cooperative learning strategies were reported to be used twice a week or more. Conversely, independent study and flexible grouping based on learning style and interests were reported to be used twice a year or less.

With LD, teachers reported using graphic organizers and varied instructional materials twice a week or more. Conversely, interest centers and learning contracts were reported to be used twice a year or less.

Feelings of Self-Efficacy

When asked to indicate their opinion about their self-efficacy in the classroom, the majority of all teachers surveyed believed that they could do a great deal to help their students value learning (67 percent) and help students believe they could do well in schoolwork (70 percent).

In order to find out if there was a difference between participants who graduated from the partnership university and participants who graduated from another university, data were compared across groups. Data revealed 63 percent of partnership-university graduates reported being able to have a great deal of ability to implement alternative strategies in their classroom (Figure 9.2).

Feelings about Differentiating Instruction

When asked about how teachers felt about differentiation, a majority of all teachers reported that planning for differentiation was worth the effort and that the ability levels of students should be taken into consideration when grading. Most of the teachers surveyed (86 percent) agreed that in a differentiated room, students are more likely to be actively engaged. Differentiating instruction requires proactive planning on the part of the teacher (Tomlinson and Imbeau, 2010). Planning for differentiation draws upon a teacher's confidence in his or her content and knowledge of management systems as well as in how to use data to inform instruction (ibid.).

The research on efficacy suggests that teachers who feel supported when attaining new pedagogies are more willing to put them into practice than those without a network of support (Hoy, 2000). Of the teachers surveyed, partnership-university graduates were more likely to agree that differentiation was well worth the effort than those who did not graduate from the university.

DISCUSSION AND NEXT STEPS

The current study affirmed the value and importance of partnerships between teaching institutions and school districts. The data analysis indicates that teachers served by the university partnerships were more likely to take the needs of students into account when planning instruction, use a variety of strategies to differentiate instruction, and feel that they had an influence on their students' learning.

The use of partnerships to provide extended professional development both during pre-service and in-service years provides teachers with the vicarious and mastery experiences needed to affirm efficacy in meeting the needs of diverse students. These findings support the original Holmes Partnership goals and have important implications for the use of partnerships in teacher-education programs in the future.

To encourage and sustain collaboration both within and without the teacher-preparation program, universities can follow many of the recommendations stemming from this study. The participants from the university partnership programs highlighted the need for (a) high-quality professional preparation, (b) training on differentiated instruction, and (c) collaboration with partnership schools.

High-Quality Preparation

Partnerships should encourage high-quality professional preparation (Holmes Group, 1995). The survey demonstrated that teachers served by university partnerships were more likely to differentiate tasks for students according to their needs and had more feelings of confidence that their efforts made a difference.

In one question, teachers were asked, "How much can you assist families in their helping their children do well in school?" Teachers were asked to select from the categories *nothing, very little, some influence, quite a bit*, or *a great deal*. Teachers who were graduates from the university where partnerships were in place were two times more likely to answer "quite a bit" or "a great deal" as compared to teachers who were graduates of other institutions.

The preparation experienced by teachers in the universities where partnerships were in place provided them an opportunity to develop their expertise through an additional endorsement program while they were pursuing their teaching certificate. They were allowed to extend their knowledge of their students by choosing between an ESL endorsement or a special education license.

University courses in meeting the needs of students with special needs are one avenue to provide vicarious experiences for building self-efficacy. To maintain the benefit of this type of training, it is worth mentioning that when a credible model teaches well, the efficacy of the observer is enhanced (Bandura, 1977). Having trained professionals deliver high-quality professional development increases the potential for impacting efficacy.

The Role of Differentiation

In this study, teachers were asked about strategies for meeting the needs of diverse learners. Teachers from the university-partnership school were more likely to characterize their knowledge of differentiation as impacting their ability to meet the needs of their students.

As teachers seek to meet the needs of students with a wide range of academic, cultural, linguistic, and emotional needs, they need a way of thinking about teaching and learning that can help them accommodate those needs. Differentiated instruction is a model that guides instructional planning in response to students' needs. Tomlinson and Imbeau (2010) note, "Differentiation can be accurately described as classroom practice with a balanced emphasis on individual students and course content" (p. 17).

Although many teachers in this study received specific training in ESL and SPED strategies, all students from the university partnership school received a course on differentiated instruction. They were more familiar with strategies and techniques for adjusting instruction for readiness, interest, and learning profile. A recommendation from this study would be to provide training in differentiation to all teacher candidates in order to build skills that will impact their capacity for mastery experiences leading to efficacy.

Collaboration with Partnership Schools

Goddard, Hoy, and Woolfolk Hoy (2000) support the idea that through improved individual teacher efficacy, the entire culture of the organization prospers. Collaboration promotes teacher efficacy, and in turn, teacher efficacy promotes collaboration. As noted earlier, the Holmes Partnership promotes simultaneous renewal, meaning that universities, schools, and professional organizations should work together to educate teachers (Holmes Group, 1995). Through work with the university programs of special education and English as a second language, this study found evidence of educators feeling confident about meeting the needs of diverse students. In particular, teachers who were graduates of the university were more likely to use a variety of instructional strategies twice a week or more. A recommendation from this study supports universities providing training both in pre-service and in-service settings to actively work on equity, diversity, and cultural competence in the education profession. Helping teacher candidates move from being consumers of knowledge to co-creators of knowledge leads to the promotion of InTASC Standard #10, "taking responsibility for student learning, to collaborate with learners, families, colleagues, other school professionals, and community members" (CCSSO, 2011).

The culture of collaboration that exists between the university and partnership schools promotes teacher candidates' sense of efficacy at a time when early teaching experiences shape their feelings of efficacy. Linda's experience was a by-product of a school where partnerships matter: "*I feel as though I know what I am doing, I'm confident in my role, and I finally feel like I am doing a good job!*"

With the intentional collaboration between university teacher-education programs, special education, ESL, and partnership schools, teacher candidates are supported as they grow in teacher efficacy.

QUESTIONS FOR TEACHER CANDIDATES, SUPERVISING TEACHERS, AND EDUCATION FACULTY

1. In what ways does your teacher-education program already build in partnerships that support teacher efficacy?
2. As you think about your current (or past) teacher-education program, who most impacted your feelings of efficacy?
3. Can you think of what partnerships might need to be built or supported to encourage the kind of collaboration that will support teacher efficacy?
4. The study noted that when teachers have competent models to learn from, they are more likely to be willing to try new pedagogies, result-

ing in increased efficacy. How might this impact the partnerships pursued by teacher-education programs?

REFERENCES

Bandura, A. (1977). Self-efficacy: Toward a unifying theory of behavioral change. *Psychological Review, 84*, 191–215.

Bandura, A. (1982). Self-efficacy mechanism in human agency. *The American Psychologist, 37*(2), 122–47.

Bandura, A. (1997). *Self-efficacy: The exercise of control.* New York, NY: W. H. Freeman and Company.

Council of Chief State School Officers (CCSSO). (2011). *The InTASC model core teaching standards.* Washington, DC: Council of Chief State School Officers.

Darling-Hammond, L., & Lieberman, A. (Eds.). (2012). *Teacher education around the world.* New York, NY: Taylor & Francis.

Goddard, R., Hoy, W., & Woolfolk Hoy, A. (2000). Collective teacher efficacy: Its meaning, measure, and impact on student achievement. *American Educational Research Journal, 37*(2), 479–507.

Goodwin, A., Smith, L., Souto-Manning, M., Cheruvu, R., Tan, M., Reed, R., & Travers, L. (2014). What should teacher educators know and be able to do? Perspectives from practicing teacher educators. *Journal of Teacher Education, 6*(4), 284–302.

Hattie, J. (2012). *Visible learning for teachers: Maximizing impact on learning.* New York, NY: Routledge.

Holmes Group (1986). *Tomorrow's Teachers.* East Lansing, MI: Holmes Group.

Holmes Group (1995). *Tomorrow's Schools of Education.* East Lansing, MI: Holmes Group.

Hoy, A. (2000, April). *The changes in teacher efficacy during the early years of teaching.* Paper presented at the meeting of the American Educational Research Association, New Orleans, LA.

Hoy, A. W., & Spero, R. B. (2005). Changes in teacher efficacy during the early years of teaching: A comparison of four measures. *Teaching and Teacher Education, 21*, 343–56.

Kennedy, S. Y., & Smith, J. B. (2013). The relationship between school collective reflective practice and teacher physiological efficacy sources. *Teaching and Teacher Education, 29*, 132–43.

Moon, T., Tomlinson, C., & Callahan, C. (1995). *Academic diversity in the middle school: Results of a national survey of middle school administrators and teachers* (Research Monograph 95124). Charlottesville, VA: National Research Center on the Gifted and Talented, University of Virginia.

Mulholland, J., & Wallace, J. (2001). Teacher induction and elementary science teaching: Enhancing self-efficacy. *Teaching and Teacher Education, 17*, 243–61.

National Commission on Excellence in Education (1983). *A nation at risk: The imperative for educational reform.* Washington, DC: U.S. Department of Education.

Tomlinson, C.A., & Imbeau, M. B. (2010). *Leading and managing a differentiated classroom.* Alexandria, VA: ASCD.

U. S. Department of Education. (n.d.). *IDEA Data Accountability Center.* Retrieved from http://www.ideadata.org.

Westberg, K. L., Archambault, F. X., Dobyns, S., & Slavin, T. (1993). *An observational study of instructional and curricular practices used with gifted and talented students in regular 120 classrooms* (Research Monograph No. 93104). Storrs: University of Connecticut, National Research Center on the Gifted and Talented.

Westberg, K., & Daoust, M. (2003, Fall). The results of the replication of the classroom practices survey replication in two states. *National Research Center on the Gifted and Talented Newsletter* (pp. 3–8).

Woolfolk Hoy, A. (2003–2004). Self-efficacy in college teaching. *Essays on Teaching Excellence: Toward the Best in the Academy, 15*(7).

Chapter Ten

Collegiality

The Practical Implications of Teacher Self-Efficacy on Collegiality, Collective Efficacy, and Student Achievement

Molly Funk

It was during my final year as a school administrator, and during the second year of implementation of a new teacher-evaluation system, when I began meeting with teachers to discuss student data and to determine the "Student Growth" portion of their evaluation. I was meeting with Wafa, a third-grade teacher, reviewing her students' reading scores. As we looked at each student individually, she talked about his or her strengths and the challenges he or she overcame during the year. This list of twenty-eight students included eight mainstreamed special education students and multiple students receiving Tier II and Tier III intervention services.

During our conversation, Wafa also consistently mentioned support she received from her grade-level colleagues with planning and adapting her instruction to meet the needs of each student. She specifically discussed the collaboration of the team with the Resource Room teacher, Amanda, and the collegiality they had developed while co-teaching the students. When we were finished calculating the growth of the students, we were in awe. One hundred percent of the students in the class made one year of growth or more. More amazingly, all eight of the identified students receiving special education services made at least two years of growth.

As we stared at this real piece of evidence of student learning, Wafa paid homage to the teachers she had the opportunity to collaborate with every day for the success in her classroom. After we analyzed and discussed the results with each of the other teachers in Wafa's grade-level team, including Aman-

da, the collegiality and collective efficacy surfaced as the cause of similar results for each of the teachers. All of their data were similar in nature. And finally, these student growth results and the high level of collegiality led each of them to receive a "Distinguished" rating on the Charlotte Danielson Framework for Teacher Evaluation.

INTRODUCTION

In today's educational world of high-stakes reform, administrators are focused on two outcomes: (1) increased teacher effectiveness and (2) increased student achievement (Fullan, 2014). Teachers are balancing initiatives such as the Common Core State Standards and state aligned tests, along with teaching the curriculum, providing interventions for struggling students, and monitoring student growth. No Child Left Behind and Race to the Top have brought about increased measures of accountability. Teachers need to not only have the skills for educating each child but also the belief that he or she can make a difference in students' learning.

Efficacious teachers look to fulfill their responsibility to each student every day in their classrooms. In the uncertainty of today's educational environment, collective teacher efficacy is extremely important. As seen with Wafa, her efficacy superseded all of the challenges she was given, and she and her colleagues shared the responsibility for each student's learning. Behavior is based on both outcome expectancy and self-efficacy (Bandura, 1977). Behavior is enacted when people not only expect certain behaviors to produce desirable outcomes (outcome expectancy), but they also believe in their own ability to perform the behaviors (self-efficacy).

TEACHER EFFICACY

Teacher efficacy is "teachers' belief or conviction that they can influence how well students learn, even those who may be difficult or unmotivated" (Guskey & Passaro, 1994 p. 4). Berman and McLaughlin (1978) describe teacher efficacy as "the extent to which the teacher believes he or she has the capacity to affect student performance" (p. 47). According to Brophy and Evertson (1977) as cited in Gibson and Dembo (1984):

> Teachers who were successful in producing student learning gains in the Texas Teacher Effectiveness Study tended to have higher expectations and assumed personal responsibility for making sure that students learned. If these teachers encountered difficulties, they viewed them as obstacles to be overcome by discovering appropriate teaching methods, not as indicators that the students could not learn. (p. 174)

Teachers who believe that all students can learn have high teacher efficacy. Teacher efficacy can be observed in the daily classroom instructional practices and learning activities of these teachers. School administrators can easily identify teachers with high efficacy by the conversations they have surrounding student learning. These teachers are reflective in nature, looking for different ways to teach students who were unable to show achievement gains in an area after their teaching.

Self-efficacy is a crucial attribute of teachers as they embark on the movement of Multi-Tiered Systems of Support (MTSS). In MTSS, teachers are responsible for identifying students with the greatest needs and providing differentiated instruction. A teacher's confidence in their teaching ability and the students' ability to learn is indicative of whether the teacher will work with a student through a failure situation in the classroom (Good, 1982, as cited in Gibson & Dembo, 1984). It is a necessity that students who need MTSS and special education programs have a teacher who believes they can learn and who is committed to making that happen.

Peter Senge, professor at MIT and leader in Organizational Learning, was interviewed in 1995. He was asked to give suggestions about transforming a school into a learning organization if he were the principal. He indicated he would "find the teachers who were interested in doing things differently, who have some real commitment and passion to do it, and get them talking to each other" (p. 21). Additionally, he says that "starting with the 'starters' is practical. Nothing in schools or other organizations will change unless individuals' beliefs, ways of seeing the world, skills, and capabilities are given an environment conducive to change" (p. 22).

Teachers' beliefs about how students can learn and about their own teaching practices are what shift when teacher efficacy is increased. Senge (1995) suggested that we start with the teachers with high efficacy and strategically create environments where they can persuade and enable efficacy in their colleagues. According to Rosenholz (1989), teacher collaboration is linked to higher teacher efficacy.

Teacher efficacy is based on Bandura's social cognitive theory (1986; 1997). He identified four sources of self-efficacy information: mastery experience, vicarious experience, social persuasion, and emotional arousal.

Mastery experience. Mastery experiences are important for organizations. As a group, teachers experience successes and failures. Mastery experiences contain efficacy-building experiences through thoughtfully designed staff development activities and action research. The earlier in their career teachers can experience mastery experiences and have successes in their classrooms, the higher their self-efficacy tends to be. (Elliot, Isaacs, & Chugani, 2010)

Vicarious experience. Teachers do not need direct experiences as the only source of collective efficacy. They listen to stories about achievements of their

colleagues as well as success stories of other schools. They include professional learning communities (PLCs) where teachers talk about successful student
achievement experiences. According to Olson and Craig (2001) "Teachers
share stories of practice in safe places, that is, knowledge communities." (p.
669)

Social persuasion. The more cohesive the faculty, the more likely they are to
be persuaded by sound argument. Persuasion can encourage a faculty to give
the extra effort that leads to success; thus, persuasion can support persistence,
and persistence can lead to the solution of problems. Talks, workshops, professional development opportunities, and feedback about achievement can influence teachers.

Affective states. Organizations react to stress just as individuals do. Efficacious
organizations can tolerate pressure and crises and continue to function without
severe negative consequences. The level of professional dialogue among
teachers with high level of efficacy changes. Wignall (1992) says that "teachers tolerate (even encourage) debate, discussion and disagreement. They are
comfortable sharing both their successes and their failures. They praise and
recognize one another's triumphs, and offer empathy and support for each
other's troubles." (p. 5)

If schools plan and implement collegial professional learning experiences
among teachers, they stand to increase teacher efficacy (Darling-Hammond
& McLaughlin, 1995; Holloway, 2003). Moreover, collegial opportunities
will provide the *vicarious experience, social persuasion,* and *affective states*
Bandura (1986; 1997) describes. Training programs, observing highly self-
efficacious teachers, and a sense of school community increases teacher self-
efficacy.

When collegial, trusting professional learning communities are in place,
the groundwork has been laid for teachers to use opportunities from their
professional learning activities. These teachers are also more likely to be
willing to try new ideas in their classrooms and engage in professional experimentation with instructional methods in order to best meet the needs of their
students (Berman & McLaughlin, 1978; Guskey, 1988).

The implementation of programs and teaching methods in classrooms
may depend on the collaboration of teachers about classroom teaching practices. As seen with Wafa and Amanda's co-teaching relationship, observing
and learning from colleagues plays a critical role in helping children learn.
Labone (2004) believed teacher self-efficacy would grow from increases in
frequency and quality of teacher collegial interaction and observation. Professional learning communities foster cultures where teachers feel safe to use
"visitation and review of each teacher's classroom behavior by peers as a
feedback and assistance activity" (Hord, 1997, p. 18).

PROFESSIONAL LEARNING COMMUNITIES

The term *professional learning community* is widely used and misappropriated in schools to describe various meetings of individuals. The big idea behind professional learning communities is the shift in focus for educators from teaching to learning (DuFour, 2004). Teachers must become comfortable with a shift of control in the classroom. DuFour identifies three crucial questions to drive the work of those within a PLC:

- What do we want each student to learn?
- How will we know when each student has learned it?
- How will we respond when a student experiences difficulty or excels in learning?

It is noticeable that the questions driving the discussions in professional learning communities are student-learning centered with a focus on reflective teaching. Also, *we* implies that it is a collective effort to facilitate learning for all students, even those who are not achieving the learning standard. Teachers are concerned with the learning outcomes of all students and design instruction to reach learners at all levels.

Hord (1997, p. 6) says that a community in which the teachers in a school and its administrators continuously seek and share learning, and act on their learning, is a PLC. Additionally, she determines that the goal of these communities is for teachers to work collaboratively to become more effective in order to have the greatest benefit for students. Collaborative planning and teaching offers students the best use of resources in the school setting.

Literature about professional development for teachers advocates that creating networks for teachers to work collegially and interact with their colleagues is critical for teachers' professional growth (Garet et al., 2001). The participation of teachers in professional learning communities is most beneficial when it is integrated into the school schedule (Darling-Hammond & McLaughlin, 1995) and has "collective participation of teachers from the same school, department, or grade" (Desimone et al., 2002, p. 102). Hord (1997) acknowledges Ernest Boyer's research (1995), where he concluded:

> The most essential factor in a successful school is that of *connection*; the most successful learning occurs when teachers teach effectively in their own classrooms but also find solutions *together*. In such schools, teachers operate as team members, with shared goals and time routinely designated for professional collaboration. Under these conditions, teachers are more likely to be consistently well informed, professionally renewed, and inspired so that they inspire students. (pp. 23–24)

Professional learning communities provide teachers with the opportunities to have substantive conversations about teaching and learning. Through high-quality deliberation, discussion, and protocols, including reading and journal writing, teachers have the opportunity through professional development to become reflective practitioners (Clift, Houston, & Pugach, 1990; Cruickshank, 1990). In PLCs, teachers engage in ongoing discussions that promote team learning by analyzing classroom practices for the purpose of improvement. The professional learning community process leads to higher levels of student achievement (DuFour, 2004).

Professional learning communities put systems in place for schools to collaborate in a student-achievement-centered conversation. In reference to Darling-Hammond's presentation of her paper (1992), Hord (1997) relayed that opportunities are needed for teachers to share knowledge and consult about the problems and challenges that arise when teaching. If not planned and scheduled, these types of conversations are left to serendipitous chance. Student achievement, the primary outcome of teaching, is necessary and cannot be left to such chance.

COLLECTIVE EFFICACY

School administrators need to look for new ways to address the issues of teacher practice in their classrooms. There is a distinction between general efficacy, which are factors beyond a teacher's control, and personal efficacy, which are a teacher's personal factors. Goddard, Hoy, and Hoy (2000) also compare individual teacher efficacy with collective teacher efficacy as follows:

> Just as individual teacher efficacy may partially explain the effect of teachers on student achievement, from an organizational perspective, collective teacher efficacy may help to explain the differential effect that schools have on student achievement. Collective teacher efficacy, therefore, has the potential to contribute to our understanding of how schools differ in the attainment of their most important objective—the education of students. (p. 7)

Professional development and professional learning communities may provide the necessary systems to achieve collective teacher efficacy. As described by Goddard, Hoy, and Hoy (2004), collective teacher efficacy beliefs are the perceptions of teachers in a school that the faculty as a whole can organize and then execute a course of action required to have a positive effect on students. School administrators need to foster this type of collaborative environment.

The literature identifies the value of a culture that embraces collegiality. According to Little (1982), in these cultures, teachers frequently engage in explicit and precise talk about their instructional practice. He also suggests that collegial teachers embrace the processes of planning, designing, researching, evaluating, and preparing teaching material and instruction together. "Teachers teach each other the practice of teaching" (p. 331).

An overarching theme indicated in the literature was that collegiality and a shared learning community was an effective method of professional development. The American Educational Research Association (AERA, 2005) reported that professional development leads to improved student learning when it connects to content knowledge, collective participation, and active learning. This is because the more time teachers spend on professional learning, the more significantly they adjust their practices. Professional learning communities are a vehicle for schools to optimize the time spent on professional development.

CONCLUSION

Creating cultures of ongoing learning and professional practice are part of the growth of a school organization to implement change in teacher practices in the classroom. Cultures of support for professional learning, including professional learning communities, are beneficial for teachers as well. Rosenholtz and Smylie (1984) advise that "increasing teacher effectiveness with students through opportunities for professional growth was the most compelling reason for teachers to remain in teaching" (p. 160).

For Wafa, Amanda, and their grade-level team, their collective effort and efficacy resulted in increased teacher effectiveness *and* increased student achievement. Their PLC collectively focused on the right discussions of student learning to best meet the needs of the students they served. Schools that can retain teachers with high teacher efficacy have the potential to create organizations of continuous learning and growth for the benefit of students. Therefore, schools have the potential to create cultures that support and foster not only individual teacher efficacy but also collective teacher efficacy and collegiality.

DISCUSSION QUESTIONS

1. In what ways do you/might you intentionally create collegial conversations with your teacher colleagues?
2. How might you use the information in this chapter to support a resistant colleague to work in PLCs?
3. Some teachers feel that the high-stakes evaluation processes have "disabled" teacher collegiality, pitting them against one another. How

might you use the information about collective efficacy to discuss this topic with your colleagues?

4. What might be some ways you could use the example of collegiality and collective efficacy to show how collective efficacy could impact student achievement in your school?

RESOURCES

Learning Forward. http://learningforward.org.

Learning by Doing: A Handbook for Professional Learning Communities at Work (2006), Richard DuFour and Rebecca DuFour. http://www.solution-tree.com/learning-by-doing.html.

Learning by Doing Study Guide. http://pages.solution-tree.com/rs/solutiontree/images/LBD_StudyGuide.pdf%20.

What Works in Schools: Translating Research into Action (2003), Robert Marzano. http://www.ascd.org/publications/books/102271.aspx.

What Works in Schools—Resources. http://www.ascd.org/research-a-topic/what-works-in-schools-resources.aspx.

Building Teachers' Capacity for Success: A Collaborative Approach for Coaches and School Leaders (2008), Pete Hall and Alisa Simeral. http://www.ascd.org/publications/books/109002.aspx.

Building Teachers' Capacity for Success—Study Guide. http://www.ascd.org/publications/books/109002/chapters/An-ASCD-Study-Guide-for-Building-Teachers'-Capacity-for-Success.aspx.

The Principal: Three Keys to Maximizing Impact (2008), Michael Fullan. http://josseybasseducation.com/teaching-learning/michael-fullans-new-book-principal-excerpt/.

The Principal: Three Keys Handouts. http://www.michaelfullan.ca/wp-content/uploads/2014/05/14_The-Principal-Handout_Spring-Summer.pdf.

Professional Capital: Transforming Teaching in Every School (2012), Andy Hargreaves and Michael Fullan. http://store.tcpress.com/0807753327.shtml.

Professional Capital Article by Fullan. http://www.michaelfullan.ca/wp-content/uploads/2013/08/JSD-Power-of-Professional-Capital.pdf.

REFERENCES

American Educational Research Association. (2005). Teaching teachers: Professional development to improve student achievement. *Research Points, 3*(1), 1–4.

Bandura, A. (1986). *Social foundations of thought and action: A social cognitive theory.* Englewood Cliffs, NJ: Prentice-Hall.

Bandura, A. (1993). Perceived self-efficacy in cognitive development and functioning. *Educational Psychologist, 28*(2), 117–48.

Bandura, A. (1997). *Self-efficacy: The exercise of control.* New York, NY: W. H. Freeman.

Berman, P., & McLaughlin, M. W. (1978). *Federal programs supporting educational change, Vol. VIII: Implementing and sustaining innovations.* Santa Monica, CA: Rand Corporation.

Clift, R. T., Houston, W. R., & Pugach, M. C. (1990). *Encouraging reflective practice in Education.* New York, NY: Teachers College Press.

Cruickshank, D. R. (1990). *Reflective teaching: The preparation of students of teaching.* Reston, VA: Association of Teacher Educators.

Darling-Hammond, L. (1992, June). Reframing the school reform agenda. *Phi Delta Kappan, 74*(10), 752–61. Paper presented at the annual meeting of the American Educational Research Association. San Francisco, April 20–24, 1992.

Darling-Hammond, L., & McLaughlin, M. (1995). Policies that support professional development in an era of reform. *Phi Delta Kappan, 76*(1), 597–603.

Desimone, L. M., Porter, A. C., Garet, M. S., Yoon, K. S., & Birman, B. F. (2002). Effects of professional development on teachers' instruction: Results from a three-year longitudinal study. *Educational Evaluation and Policy Analysis, 24*(2), 81–112.

DuFour, R. (2004). What is a "professional learning community"? *Educational Leadership, 61*(8), 6–11.

Elliott, E. M, Isaacs, M. L., & Chugani, C. D. (2010). Promoting self-efficacy in early career teachers: A principal's guide for differentiated mentoring and supervision. *Florida Journal of Educational Administration & Policy, 4*(1), 131–46.

Fullan, M. (2014). *The Principal: Three keys to maximizing impact.* San Francisco, CA: Jossey-Bass.

Garet, M. S., Porter, A. C., Desimone, L., Birman, B. F., & Yoon, K. S. (2001). What makes professional development effective? Results from a national sample of teachers. *American Educational Research Journal, 38*(4), 915–45.

Gibson, S., & Dembo, M. (1984). Teacher efficacy: A construct validation. *Journal of Educational Psychology 76*(4), 569–82.

Goddard, R. D., Hoy, W. K., & Hoy, A. W. (2000). Collective teacher efficacy: Its meaning, measure, and impact on student achievement. *American Educational Research Journal, 37*(2), 479–507.

Goddard, R. D., Hoy, W. K., & Hoy, A. W. (2004). Collective efficacy beliefs: Theoretical developments, empirical evidence, and future directions. *Educational Researcher, 33*(3), 3–13.

Guskey, T. R. (1984). The influence of change in instructional effectiveness upon the affective characteristics of teachers. *American Educational Research Journal, 21*(2), 245–59.

Holland, H. (2005). Teaching teachers: Professional development to improve student achievement. *Research Points, 3*(1), 1–4.

Holloway, J. H. (2003). Sustaining experienced teachers. *Educational Leadership, 60*(8), 87–89.

Hord, S. M. (1997). *Professional learning communities: Communities of continuous inquiry and improvement.* Southwest Educational Development Laboratory, 211 East Seventh Street, Austin, TX 78701.

Labone, E. (2004). Teacher efficacy: Maturing the construct through research in alternative paradigms. *Teaching & Teacher Education: An International Journal of Research and Studies, 20*(4), 341–59.

Little, J. W. (1982). Norms of collegiality and experimentation: Workplace conditions of school success. *American Educational Research Journal, 19*(3), 325–40.

Olson, M. R., & Craig, C. J. (2001). Opportunities and challenges in the development of teachers' knowledge: The development of narrative authority through knowledge communities. *Teaching and Teacher Education, 17*(6), 667–84.

Rosenholz, S. (1989). *Teacher's workplace: The social organization of schools.* New York: Longman.

Rosenholtz, S. J., & Smylie, M. A. (1984). Teacher compensation and career ladders. *The Elementary School Journal, 85*(2), 149–65.

Schechter, C., & Tschannen-Moran, M. (2006). Teachers' sense of collective efficacy: An international view. *International Journal of Educational Management, 20*(6), 480–89.

Senge, P. (1995). In on schools as learning organizations: A conversation with Peter Senge. *Educational Leadership, 52*(7).

Wignall, R. (1992). Building a collaborative school culture: A case study of one woman in the principalship. In *European Conference on Educational Research,* Enschede, The Netherlands.

Final Thoughts

As evidenced by the chapters in this book, self-efficacy is not a magical milestone to be reached or a box to be checked when completed. It is an ever-evolving process experienced by individuals as they move through their professional careers. Some appear to start their teaching careers with an abundance of self-efficacy. They seem to effortlessly make decisions and handle situations in their classrooms with the greatest of ease. This is often intimidating to colleagues who struggle with whether they have made the right decisions and with taking charge of enacting classroom changes. Regardless of where each of us lands on the continuum, self-efficacy can improve with each situation encountered and successfully handled. Even those who are naturally self-efficacious will encounter situations where they must search for the correct responses and must reflect on their actions and decisions to make the best choices for student success and satisfaction.

A significant aspect of developing self-efficacy is reflection on decisions. Is this a good course of action? Is this the best decision for students? Did this work, or how can it be improved? Another aspect of developing self-efficacy is giving ourselves credit when we do show evidence of self-efficacy with students and in professional roles. There will always be doubt on whether the very best decision was made, but we should celebrate our success and acknowledge when we "get it right" with our students.

As we gain metacognitively with regard to our own developing self-efficacy, we move from not knowing what we don't know to not consciously knowing, or thinking about, all the things we have learned along the way. Often it is only through reflection that we come to realize we are growing and becoming more skilled in our profession. Howell (1982) provides illustration of the hierarchy of personal and professional growth experiences (Figure F.1).

Four Stages of Learning

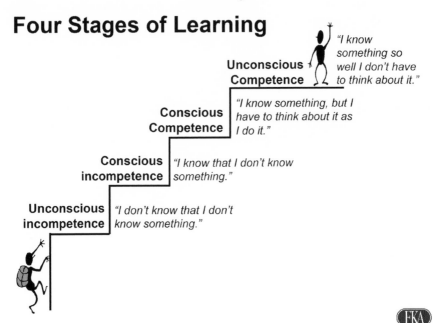

Unconscious Competence — "I know something so well I don't have to think about it."

Conscious Competence — "I know something, but I have to think about it as I do it."

Conscious incompetence — "I know that I don't know something."

Unconscious incompetence — "I don't know that I don't know something."

Figure F.1

It is not unusual to move back and forth from unconscious incompetence to conscious competence depending on the situation. Teachers are, themselves, lifelong learners. Tackling a new skill, acquiring new knowledge, developing a new lesson plan, or approaching life from a different perspective can cause a move back to unconscious incompetence. Even those with a high degree of self-efficacy will sometimes find themselves moving through a level of incompetence when faced with unfamiliar situations. The authors of the various chapters of this book contend, similarly to Mark Twain (1883), that

> two things seemed pretty apparent to us. One was that in order to be a teacher with self-efficacy a person had got to know more than any one person ought to be allowed to know; and the other was, that the teacher with self-efficacy must learn it all over again in a different way every 24 hours.

Hopefully, the chapters in this book helped you see the development of self-efficacy in characters showcased in the vignettes. From Changes in teacher candidates in a practicum experience to growth in experienced teachers, constructs such as Commitment, Community, and Control fostered development in self-efficacy. Attributes of Collegiality and Collaboration allowed teachers to work together to overcome Challenges and develop Curriculum to meet the needs of students with Care, Confidence, and Creativity.

None of the vignette characters developed all of their self-efficacy tools overnight. They moved up and down Howell's competency matrix as they acquired their skills.

As mentioned earlier, we all exhibit self-efficacy in varying degrees given our situations and personalities. Chen, Gully, and Eden (2001) offer a self-assessment that each of us should consider as we reflect on our individual levels of self-efficacy. For each of these eight items, we can rate ourselves using the levels of *strongly agree, agree, neutral, disagree,* and *strongly disagree*:

- I will be able to achieve most of the goals that I have set for myself.
- When facing difficult tasks, I am certain I will accomplish them.
- In general, I think I can obtain outcomes that are important to me.
- I believe I can be successful at almost any endeavor to which I set my mind.
- I will be able to successfully overcome many challenges.
- I am confident that I can perform effectively on many different tasks.
- Compared to other people, I can do most tasks very well.
- Even when things are tough, I can perform quite well.

From these eight items, educators can apply their insights to their personal, professional, and pedagogical energies and expertise. When the self-assessment reveals that *strongly agree* is not the response, educators can investigate their perceptions and situations to identify areas of growth and development useful across their lives as shared in the chapters of this book.

So, in sharing these final thoughts with you, we contend that one never really knows all there is to know about being a self-efficacious teacher because the people, things, and ideas of education are in a constant state of flux. But, the teacher with self-efficacy knows that and recognizes that they have to "re-learn" their respective self-efficacy strategies and methods every day in order to maintain their self-efficacy edge throughout their career. Therefore, keep on learning and teaching and learning and teaching . . .

REFERENCES

Chen, G., Gully, S. M., & Eden, D. (2001). Validation of a new general self-efficacy scale. *Organizational Research Methods, 4,* 62–83.
Howell, W. S. (1982). *The empathic communicator.* University of Minnesota: Wadsworth.
Twain, M. (1883). *Life on the Mississippi.* Boston, MA: James R. Osgood and Company.

Appendix

In 1987, the Interstate New Teacher Assessment and Support Consortium (InTASC) was launched to reform the licensing, preparation, and professional development of teachers. InTASC upholds the idea that well-trained teachers should integrate content knowledge with student requirements and specific strengths to make sure that all students are able to learn and perform well at high levels. In order to achieve these goals, InTASC has created ten different standards for novice teachers, based on the advanced certification standards of the National Board for Professional Teaching. These standards offer an in-depth view of the skills that should be demonstrated by new teachers and highlights characteristics that novice teachers must have to become successful teachers in the classroom.

Standard #1—Learner Development

The teacher candidate understands how learners grow and develop, recognizing that patterns of learning and development vary individually within and across the cognitive, linguistic, social, emotional, and physical areas, and designs and implements developmentally appropriate and challenging learning experiences.

Standard #2—Learning Differences

The teacher candidate uses understanding of individual differences and diverse cultures and communities to ensure inclusive learning environments that enable each learner to meet high standards.

Standard #3 — Learning Environments

The teacher candidate works with others to create environments that support individual and collaborative learning, and that encourage positive social interaction, active engagement in learning, and self-motivation.

Standard #4 — Content Knowledge

The teacher candidate understands the central concepts, tools of inquiry, and structures of the discipline(s) he or she teaches and creates learning experiences that make these aspects of the discipline accessible and meaningful for learners to assure mastery of the content.

Standard #5 — Application of Content

The teacher candidate understands how to connect concepts and use differing perspectives to engage learners in critical thinking, creativity, and collaborative problem solving related to authentic local and global issues.

Standard #6 — Assessment

The teacher candidate understands and uses multiple methods of assessment to engage learners in their own growth, to monitor learner progress, and to guide the teacher's and learner's decision making.

Standard #7 — Planning for Instruction

The teacher candidate plans instruction that supports every student in meeting rigorous learning goals by drawing upon knowledge of content areas, curriculum, cross-disciplinary skills, and pedagogy, as well as knowledge of learners and the community context.

Standard #8 — Instructional Strategies

The teacher candidate understands and uses a variety of instructional strategies to encourage learners to develop deep understanding of content areas and their connections, and to build skills to apply knowledge in meaningful ways.

Standard #9 — Professional Learning and Ethical Practice

The teacher candidate engages in ongoing professional learning and uses evidence to continually evaluate his/her practice, particularly the effects of his/her choices and actions on others (learners, families, other professionals, and the community), and adapts practice to meet the needs of each learner.

Standard #10—Leadership and Collaboration

The teacher candidate seeks appropriate leadership roles and opportunities to take responsibility for student learning, to collaborate with learners, families, colleagues, other school professionals, and community members to ensure learner growth, and to advance the profession.

REFERENCES

Council of Chief State School Officers (CCSSO). (2011). *Interstate Teacher Assessment and Support Consortium (InTASC) Model Core Teaching Standards: A Resource for State Dialogue.* Washington, DC: Author.

About the Authors and Editors

EDITORS

Freddie A. Bowles is associate professor of education at the University of Arkansas, Fayetteville. She is the program coordinator for the Master of Arts in Teaching Secondary Education program and specializes in foreign language education, language preservation, and multicultural issues in education.

Cathy J. Pearman is professor and department head in the College of Education at Missouri State University. Her research focus is on the self-efficacy of educators and teacher candidates, literacy assessment, and exploring effects of technology on literacy skill development and comprehension.

AUTHORS

Jennifer G. Beasley is the director of teacher education at the University of Arkansas, Fayetteville. She specializes in gifted education, curriculum, and differentiation.

Glenda L. Black is associate professor at the Schulich School of Education, Nipissing University, specializing in international practicums, indigenous education, and service-learning.

Brett Campbell is visiting associate professor of psychology at Brigham Young University. He focuses on self-efficacy in learning math and conceptual change in science.

Amanda Careena Fernandes is a teacher in Ontario. Her research focuses on the classroom environment inclusive of nonnative language learning, assessment, and pragmatic competence.

Kylie Flynn has had teaching experiences in Canada and Thailand. Her research includes investigating culturally related education and developing engaging and inclusive classrooms.

Molly Funk is an educational consultant, coach, and doctoral candidate at Eastern Michigan University. She specializes in school leadership, educator effectiveness, and early literacy.

Nancy P. Gallavan is professor of teacher education at the University of Central Arkansas where she specializes in assessment, cultural competence, and social studies education.

Ashlie R. Jack is assistant dean/accreditation officer at Wichita State University. Her research includes educator preparation, academic vocabulary, and content literacy instruction.

Elizabeth K. Johnson is professor at Eastern Michigan University, where she teaches and conducts professional development within seven Indigenous Reservation Sovereign Nations.

Suzanne H. Jones is associate professor at Utah State University. She specializes in collective classroom efficacy, emotions and learning, and conceptual change learning.

Shirley Lefever is dean of the College of Education at Wichita State University. She is also the 2016–2017 president of the Association of Teacher Educators.

Kimberly McDowell is professor and department head in curriculum and instruction at Wichita State University. She specializes in literacy, ELLs, PD, and early childhood education.

Terrell M. Peace is director of graduate/undergraduate teacher education at Huntington University. His interests are neuroscience, educational psychology, and pedagogical theory.

Walter S. Polka is professor and coordinator of the PhD Program in Leadership and Policy at Niagara University. He has multiple worldwide presentations on teaching and learning.

LeAnn G. Putney is professor of educational psychology at the University of Nevada, Las Vegas. She specializes in teaching sociocultural theory and qualitative research methods.

Elissa Good Smith is the PreK–6 principal at Lyndonville Central School in western New York. She serves as a New York Educator Voice Policy Fellow with America Achieves.

Mary Kathleen (Kathy) Walsh is president-elect of the Michigan Association of Teacher Educators and president/CEO of Extreme Teaching for Extreme Times, LLC.

Angela Webster-Smith is associate professor of leadership studies and associate vice president for institutional diversity at the University of Central Arkansas.